Constitutionalism: ANCIENT AND MODERN

Constitutionalism

ANCIENT AND MODERN

CHARLES HOWARD McILWAIN

*Eaton Professor of the Science of Government,
Emeritus, in Harvard University*

REVISED EDITION

Cornell Paperbacks

CORNELL UNIVERSITY PRESS

ITHACA AND LONDON

Published in the United Kingdom by Cornell University Press Ltd.,
London.

First Edition, 1940
Revised Edition, 1947
First printing, Great Seal Books, 1958
Second printing, 1961
Third printing, Cornell Paperbacks, 1966
Sixth printing 1983

International Standard Book Number 0-8014-9010-3
Printed in the United States of America

To the members of the Telluride Association
of Cornell University in lasting remembrance
of their friendliness and hospitality.

IN ITS ORIGINAL FORM this book consists of six lectures which the author delivered at Cornell University in the academic year 1938–39, namely, the MESSENGER LECTURES ON THE EVOLUTION OF CIVILIZATION. That series was founded and its title was prescribed by the late Hiram J. Messenger, B.Litt., Ph.D., of Hartford, Connecticut, who directed in his will that a portion of his estate be given to Cornell University and used to provide annually "a course or courses of lectures on the evolution of civilization, for the special purpose of raising the moral standard of our political, business, and social life."

Preface

THIS VOLUME, it is hardly necessary to say, does not pretend to be a comprehensive account of the growth of constitutionalism. In the course of a few lectures nothing could be attempted beyond the tracing of a very limited number of salient principles, and even these could be dealt with only for those countries where their development is most obvious and most directly related to the political problems facing us here and now. The history of constitutionalism remains to be written.

To the committee in charge of the Messenger Lectures I wish to express my deep appreciation of the honor and the opportunity of presenting this subject in this distinguished series, and to the Cornell University Press and Mr. Woodford Patterson its Director my thanks for valued advice and assistance in the preparation of the manuscript of these lectures for the press.

C. H. McILWAIN

Belmont, Massachusetts
March 2, 1940

In this revised edition many additions have been made in the notes and an appendix has been added further to justify or to illustrate some of the statements in the text.

C. H. M.

Princeton, New Jersey
May, 1947

Contents

Constitutionalism: ANCIENT AND MODERN

CHAPTER I

Some Modern Definitions
of Constitutionalism

THE TIME seems to be propitious for an examination of the general principle of constitutionalism—our own Anglo-Saxon brand of it in particular—and an examination which should include some consideration of the successive stages in its development. For perhaps never in its long history has the principle of constitutionalism been so questioned as it is questioned today, never has the attack upon it been so determined or so threatening as it is just now. The world is trembling in the balance between the orderly procedure of law and the processes of force which seem so much more quick and effective. We must make our choice between these two, and it must be made in the very near future. If we are to make that choice intelligently it would seem reasonable, whether in the end we decide for law or for force, that we should retrace the history of our constitutionalism—the history of force is plain enough —should try to estimate its past achievements, and should consider the nature and effects of the forces which have been arrayed against it. This I propose to try briefly to do and as dispassionately as I can, though it is only fair that I should frankly confess at the outset that my own personal convictions are overwhelmingly on the side of law and against force.

In 1792 Arthur Young mentions with contempt the French notion of a constitution, which, he says, "is a new term they have adopted; and which they use as if a constitution was a pudding to be made by a receipt." [1] To Thomas Paine, writing at the same time, the recent American written constitutions are "to liberty, what a grammar is to language." In another place, speaking of constitutions in general, he says: "A constitution is not the act of a government, but of a people constituting a government, and a government without a constitution is power without right." "A constitution is a thing *antecedent* to a government; and a government is only the creature of a constitution." It seems probable that Paine means by "constitution" nothing less than the written constitutions of America or France. For, he says, "the continual use of the word 'constitution' in the English parliament shows there is none; and that the whole is merely a form of government without a constitution, and constituting itself with what power it pleases." "The act by which the English parliament empowered itself to sit for seven years, shews there is no constitution in England. It might, by the same authority have sate any greater number of years, or for life." [2]

For Arthur Young, a constitution in this sense of a "written" constitution is "a new term"; for Thomas Paine it seems to be the only kind of constitution worthy of the name. Such "puddings," "made by a receipt," were to Edmund Burke apparently as repulsive as to Arthur Young. He says little or nothing about the new American constitutions, but in his opinion nothing could be worse than the French one. "What in the result is likely to produce evil, is politically false," he says; and "that which is productive of good, politically true." [3] Certainly, in his view, nothing but evil had come or could come from "that monstrous thing, which, by the courtesy of France, they call a constitution." [4]

These statements express very clearly the contrast between

2

the new conception of the conscious formulation by a people of its fundamental law, the new definition of "constitution"; and the older traditional view in which the word was applied only to the substantive principles to be deduced from a nation's actual institutions and their development. The older view was probably never better indicated than by Bolingbroke, when he said in 1733:

> By constitution we mean, whenever we speak with propriety and exactness, that assemblage of laws, institutions and customs, derived from certain fixed principles of reason, directed to certain fixed objects of public good, that compose the general system, according to which the community hath agreed to be governed. . . . We call this a good government, when . . . the whole administration of public affairs is wisely pursued, and with a strict conformity to the principles and objects of the constitution.[5]

One noteworthy difference between Paine's conception and Bolingbroke's is that for the former a governmental act contrary to the constitution is an act of "power without right"; for the latter it only warrants us in saying that that government is not a good one.

Bolingbroke in fact is only restating views as old as the *Politicus* of Plato when he says that governments may be compared and estimated by their conformity to reason, and that a nation's actual customs and laws are probably the safest actual criterion of what that reason is. If a government fails so to conform, it is a bad government, but he does not say it is without right. He does not imply, as Paine does, that it may be disobeyed, except by way of revolution. It is curious that Bolingbroke gives the same illustration as Paine of what we might call an "unconstitutional" enactment, the English Septennial Act of 1716. That statute Paine considered a conclusive

3

proof that "there is no constitution in England." Bolingbroke's remarks about the same statute are interesting both for what he says and for what he does not say:

If it had been foretold to those patriots at the revolution, who remembered long parliaments, who still felt the smart of them, who struggled hard for annual, and obtained with much difficulty, at the end of five or six years, triennial parliaments, that a time would come when even the term of triennial parliaments would be deemed too short, and a parliament chosen for three years would choose itself for four more, and entail septennial parliaments on the nation; that this would happen, and the fruits of their honest labors be lost, in little more than twenty years; and that it would be brought about, whilst our government continued on the foundations they had then so newly laid: if all this had been foretold at the time I mention, it would have appeared improbable and monstrous to the friends of the revolution. Yet it hath happened; and in less than twenty years, it is grown, or is growing, familiar to us.[6]

When Burke appealed from the new to the old Whigs in 1791 it was the conservatism of 1689 to which he would have returned, in place of the more radical views of Fox. When Bolingbroke in 1733 says that the Septennial Act would have seemed "monstrous" to the Whigs of the Revolution, it is in reaction against the arbitrariness of the growing notion of the omnipotence of parliament. To the one the new Whigs had moved too far toward the left, as we should say; to the other they were already moving too far toward the very absolutism their predecessors had fought against. Bolingbroke's statement is interesting in more ways than one. He offers no legal remedy for the abuse of which he complains, but he does see, as some modern historians have not seen, that between the Whig doctrine of 1689 and that of the reign of George III, or even of George I, a great gulf yawns. The opponents of James II had

4

declared that the throne was vacant only by virtue of the fact that their voice was assumed to be the voice of the nation. In 1766 Lord Chancellor Northington said in course of the debate on the repeal of the Stamp Act: "Every *government* can *arbitrarily* impose laws on all its subjects; there must be a supreme dominion in every state; whether monarchical, aristocratical, democratical, or mixed. And all the subjects of each state are bound by the laws made by government." [7]

In 1791 Burke, though opposing the extreme doctrines of the radicals, expressly reiterated his earlier belief that the Americans in their rebellion against England had stood "in the same relation to England, as England did to King James the second, in 1688." [8]

Illustrations of the changing conceptions of sovereignty and of the constitution could be multiplied indefinitely from the materials of the seventeenth and eighteenth centuries. In contrasting the "monstrous" theory of the Septennial Act with that of the original Whig instigators of the Revolution, Bolingbroke implies that the latter, in the Convention Parliament, were acting not as a body with inherent, arbitrary, sovereign authority; but merely as the voice of the whole people. In the Whig pamphlets of the revolutionary period there is a good deal of evidence to confirm this view. The Lords in the Convention Parliament had called that assembly "a full and free Representative of this Nation" [9] and there were some who recognized, on Locke's principles, that it was a purely extra-legal and revolutionary body whose acts were not legislative but constituent. In one of the ablest of the pamphlets of the time [10] it is recognized that there is no adequate remedy in law for the abuses complained of, because many of James's most oppressive acts had been strictly legal. "This I think may easily be granted," the author says,

5

if it be consider'd, That the present Laws and Constitutions of England are such as do undoubtedly give the King a Power to make the Judg, and to the Judg a Power to pronounce the law. What he does judicially affirm, is Law, and becomes from thenceforth the strongest Precedent; the last Judgment being always esteem'd the surest and best Rule to go by. Now the King in both these Transactions, neither made or turn'd out any Judges, but in such Methods that former Judges had pronounc'd Lawful; nor did he do afterwards any thing either in the case of *Magdalen* College, or in the dispensing Power, but with the Opinion and Concurrence of his Judges, being the Method that our Establishment and Laws in such Cases do direct.

"No, no," he exclaims,

Tho our King was misguided, and our Judges were corrupt, yet it is not at their doors we must lay our Misfortunes, but to the weakness of our Government, which gives a Loose to these Inconveniencies, and which pins the Justice of the Nation on the Frailties of a single Man in so arbitrary a manner.

"If," he concludes,

the Departure of the King amounts to such a Desertion as dissolves the Government, then the Power must necessarily revert and vest in the People, who may erect a new one, either according to the old *Model*, if they like it so well, or any other that they like and approve of better.

The same idea was expressed by another writer [11] when he said:

These Conventions then of the two Kingdoms are Representatives of the Body Politick of the respective Kingdoms, such as might have been before these Bodies Politick enter'd into a Rectoral Contract with the first of the Kings of the Race that now reigns; and they are no Judicial or Authoritative Judicatures, and I suppose

6

will claim no Power to make Laws, to judg persons, or to impose Taxes.

In due course, like the Convention Parliament of 1660, this Convention was declared to be a parliament in words copied from the similar act at the Restoration; but in thus choosing the "old Model" instead of a new, there is no indication that the representatives of the "Body Politick" ever actually conferred, or ever thought of conferring on themselves as the new parliament, any legal authority not enjoyed by prerevolutionary parliaments. It will be necessary later to show that the authority of these earlier parliaments had never been an arbitrary one.

If then Bolingbroke is right in what he says of the Septennial Act, if that statute would have seemed nothing less than "monstrous" to the revolutionists of 1688, it seems clear that to those revolutionists the dictum of Northington and Mansfield in 1766, so strenuously opposed by Camden and the Americans at the time, that "every *government* can *arbitrarily* impose laws on all its subjects," would have been tenfold more monstrous. In fact, on the basis of this and other evidence, it seems no exaggeration to say that the Whig theory of the state after 1760 is hardly to be distinguished from the principles of James II which had brought on the Revolution of 1688. In one, as in the other, the government assumed authority to impose laws *arbitrarily*. The only difference lay in the fact that in the one case this arbitrary government was under control of an unreformed parliament and that in the other it was dominated by the will of a despotic king. Even the conservative Burke was candid enough as late as 1791 to admit that Englishmen of North America who in 1775 rebelled against such an arbitrary rule "stood in the same relation to England as England

7

did to King James the second in 1688." If the principles of 1688 had persisted unchanged, one might well doubt whether there would ever have been an American Revolution.

Against the principles of 1766 a revolt was as nearly inevitable in America as the Revolution of 1688 had been in England. Consideration of these changes brings up the nice question whether the Americans were legally or constitutionally warranted in resisting this "monstrous" doctrine just because it was grown or was growing "familiar" to Englishmen in England by 1733 and afterward—though not necessarily in America. It is a very nice question indeed, and most recent American historians of our Revolution have apparently refused to follow me in an inclination—which, nevertheless, I still feel—to prefer the contention of Camden and the Americans, even on its strictly legal side, to that of Northington and Mansfield. Viewed from the more general standpoint of politics rather than of law, this contention has been less questioned, and there is almost a consensus that it undoubtedly justified political revolution even if not legal resistance. It is with this political aspect of the question that we are immediately concerned here, for it was these political developments which lay behind and beneath the changing conception of what any constitution was or should be. Paine, in saying that a constitution must always be antecedent to any rightful government, was laying down a political maxim, not a rule of English law.

And whether we subscribe or not to the characterization of Thomas Paine by a former President of the United States as "a dirty little atheist," in which every single item seems to be inaccurate, we must, I think, at least agree that the analysis Paine made of the early American constitution was remarkably acute. The significant points in that analysis are these:

8

That there is a fundamental difference between a people's government and that people's constitution, whether the government happens to be entrusted to a king or to a representative assembly.

That this constitution is "antecedent" to the government.

That it defines the authority which the people commits to its government, and in so doing thereby limits it.

That any exercise of authority beyond these limits by any government is an exercise of "power without right."

That in any state in which the distinction is not actually observed between the constitution and the government there is in reality no constitution, because the will of the government has no check upon it, and that state is in fact a despotism.

One thing alone Paine fails to make fully clear. If a government exercises some "power without right," it seems to be necessarily implied that the people have a corresponding right to resist. But is this a legal or is it only a political right? Is such resistance a legalized rebellion or merely an extralegal revolution? Or, further, is it possible to incorporate in the framework of the state itself some provision or institution by which a governmental act or command *ultra vires* may be declared to be such, and subjects therefore exempted from its operation and released from any legal obligation to observe or obey it? In short, can government be limited legally and effectively by any method short of force? To these questions Paine gives no clear answer. It might be assumed that forcible resistance to power without right must itself be legal and not revolutionary; but in every case there seems no recourse except to force of some kind.

The one conspicuous element lacking in Paine's construction therefore seems to be the element of judicial review. Writing when he did, and as he did, to justify an actual rebel-

9

lion, it is perhaps not strange that he was thinking primarily of politics rather than of law, that the "rights" he had in mind were the rights of man rather than the rights of the citizen, or that the sanction for these rights should be extralegal action rather than any constitutional check. Paine, like many idealists in a hurry, was probably impatient of the slowness of legal remedies for existing abuses. But others, who were more constitutionally minded than he, had begun to feel that any such remedies, to be truly effective, must ultimately have the sanction of law. Years before, Lord Camden had insisted that the principles of the law of nature must be incorporated in the British Constitution if they were to be observed, and that they actually were so incorporated. The necessary inference from such a principle as his is that the interpreters of law should be the ones to define the rights of individuals and to trace the bounds of legitimate government over them. The protection of rights became for him, and for all who thought as he did, the enforcement of "constitutional limitations." In America this had been vaguely felt long before Paine wrote his *Rights of Man* or even his *Common Sense*. In 1764 James Otis, in his *Rights of the British Colonies Asserted and Proved,* had said: "If the supreme legislative errs, it is informed by the supreme executive in the King's courts of law. . . . This is government! This is a constitution." [12] In 1771 a remarkable instance occurs in the first of the sermons preached in the Old South Church in Boston on the anniversary of the so-called Boston Massacre. In it the preacher, the Reverend James Lovell, speaking of the king of England, said:

He is gracious, but not omniscient. He is ready to hear our *appeals* in their proper course: and knowing himself, though the most powerful prince on earth, yet, a subject under a divine constitution

10

of *Law;* that law he *will* ask and receive from the twelve judges of *England.* These will prove that the claim of the British parliament over *us* is not only *illegal in itself, but a downright usurpation of his prerogative* as King of *America.*[13]

This notion of the necessity in a constitutional state for a judicial interpretation and limitation of the acts of government was at first naturally vague and instinctive; it became fully and consciously developed only at a later date.

There is, however, another important side of Paine's conception of a constitution in which it might seem to differ fundamentally from the views of other opponents of arbitrary government in his own time and before. One of Paine's most fundamental assertions is that a true constitution is always *antecedent* to the actual government in a state. If by the word "antecedent" he means prior in time, he seems to be asserting a principle which can be true only of constitutions "struck off" consciously by a people at a definite time, as they had lately been formulated in the thirteen colonies in America. On such an assumption the only true constitution would appear to be a "written constitution" of a type familiar enough to us since 1776, but scarcely thought of before, except perhaps for a dozen years in the middle of the seventeenth century in England. This narrow and novel definition of a constitution may have been the one Paine had in mind, and the prominence in his political thought of the notion of a definite historical compact between the government and the governed makes it the more probable.

Antecedent, however, might well have been used by other men with a far different meaning. The quotation from Bolingbroke given above makes it evident that for him the principles of the Constitution stand before all acts of any government,

11

not because they are prior to them in time, but because they are superior in character and in binding authority; and the same was certainly true of Burke. In fact, the traditional notion of constitutionalism before the late eighteenth century was of a set of principles embodied in the institutions of a nation and neither external to these nor in existence prior to them. A constitutional state was one that had preserved an inheritance of free institutions. Precedent was the very life of these institutions as it was of all law. It was the retention of "ancient" liberties for which liberals thought they were fighting, not the creation of new ones *a priori*.

For some of the earlier of these "liberal conservatives" the safeguarding of necessary liberties seems to have implied the preservation intact of the customary law of the nation in its entirety. Sir Edward Coke, for example, appears to have thought that nothing less than the whole body of the English common law must be kept inviolate if the liberty of the subject was to be protected against arbitrary rule. For him the whole of the common law was in a sense "fundamental." He was still thinking in medieval fashion of law as custom, and all customary law had for him a higher sanction than "legislation" of any kind. Liberty, in his mind, was far from the abstract notion of the period of the Enlightenment. It still consisted, as in earlier ages, of specific concrete rights and of the whole body of these specific rights. He thought in terms of rights, not of right; of liberties, not of liberty; and he identified these concrete liberties with franchises.[14]

In one of the speeches of James I there is an interesting illustration of this habit of thought among English common lawyers, and also of the emergence of a view that we might possibly call more modern, although its roots are very old. In 1607, contrasting the Scots with the English, the king said:

12

Their meaning in the word of Fundamentall Lawes, you shall perceive more fully hereafter, when I handle the obiection of the difference of Lawes: For they intend thereby onely those Lawes whereby confusion is avoyded, and their Kings descent mainteined, and the heritage of the succession and Monarchie, which hath bene a Kingdome, to which I am in descent, three hundreth yeeres before CHRIST: Not meaning it as you doe, of their Common Law, for they have none, but that which is called IUS REGIS.[15]

The king, in this passage, is making essentially the same distinction that we now make as a matter of course between "constitutional" and other law. In restricting this constitutional law as he did to the *jus regis* or *jus coronae* he reflects his own extreme view, or monarchy by divine right, and there were undoubtedly some precedents for so restricting it, not only in Scotland but in France and England as well. But the main point is that in this view all customary law is not equally "fundamental," that some parts of it are by their inherent character more so than others, and that these parts are the ones concerned with the supreme governmental organ of the state. While these fundamentals went no further for James than the guarantee of his own royal rights, by others they might be extended and were extended to include some limitations in the interest of subjects as well. S. R. Gardiner was of opinion that the phrase "fundamental law," as a guarantee of the rights of the subject, came into use only after the ship-money trial, but there are some rather striking even if somewhat vague instances of it that antedate this by a good many years; such, for example, as the assertion of Sir James Whitelocke in 1610 that taxation without sanction of parliament "is against the natural frame and constitution of the policy of this Kingdom, which is *Jus publicum regni,* and so subverteth the fundamental law of the realm, and induceth a new form of

13

state and government," as well as "against the municipal law of the land, which is *Jus privatum*, the law of property and of private right." [16]

From the evidence of recent times, of which I have had room for only this small number of scattered illustrative cases, one or two general principles, or tendencies rather, may, I think, be legitimately deduced; and I should like to state these in somewhat brief and summary form as the basis or starting point for the survey to follow of the long historical evolution which lies behind them.

Whatever we may think of it theoretically, Paine's notion that the only true constitution is one consciously constructed, and that a nation's government is only the creature of this constitution, conforms probably more closely than any other to the actual development in the world since the opening of the nineteenth century. Whether this construction was actually prompted in the first instance by doctrinaire political philosophers, as seems largely true in France, or by actual political experience, as the history of the time appears to indicate in the revolted North American colonies of Great Britain, it is certainly true that most subsequent constitutional developments have followed the same lines. Written constitutions creating, defining, and limiting governments since then have been the general rule in almost the whole of the constitutional world. The precedent for these, first developed in North America, was naturalized in France and from there transmitted to most of the continent of Europe, from which it has spread in our own day to much of the Orient. Even the British self-governing colonies have been deeply influenced by it.

One of the curious anomalies arising out of this development is the striking exception to it furnished by England herself, the one country above all others in which limitations on

14

government have been in more or less effective operation since medieval times. But the exception of England seems more apparent than real. The essential principles to which Burke and Camden and Otis appealed were no less constitutional because they were "unwritten"; and the true reason why England, probably the most constitutional of modern European nations, has also remained the only one whose constitution has never been embodied in a formal document, is not that she has had no constitution, as the French sometimes say, but rather that limitations on arbitrary rule have become so firmly fixed in the national tradition that no threats against them have seemed serious enough to warrant the adoption of a formal code. Since written constitutions came into vogue in the late eighteenth century, England has never experienced any of the violent changes which gave France so many successive written constitutions in the nineteenth. Yet, it might be objected, the thirteen British colonies, whose traditions were those of the mother country, did without exception adopt such written constitutions, and our federal written constitution is merely the result of them.

The answer is twofold. First, our early American written constitutions might be said with little exaggeration to consist mainly of a codification of institutions and principles long in actual force. They are far less doctrinaire or *a priori* than those of France or the rest of continental Europe. And, second, our independence constituted a break in continuity here requiring a written code, such as England has never known, at least since 1660. For even the Revolution of 1688, important as it was, made few structural changes that could be set forth in a formal document even if men had thought of it. The Bill of Rights of 1689, the Triennial Act of 1694, and the Act of Settlement of 1701, which embody nearly the whole of the revolu-

15

tion settlement which obtained the sanction of law, were enacted in the form of ordinary statutes. Nevertheless, there are
indications that these enactments were at that time thought
to be in some sense, or in some degree, fundamental. The language of the Triennial Act—that writs shall issue for the
assembling of a new parliament "within three years at the
farthest, from and after the dissolution of this present Parliament, and so from time to time *forever hereafter*"—certainly
furnishes some ground for Bolingbroke's assertion that a revolutionary change took place between 1694 and 1716 which
even the men of 1688 might have considered "monstrous." If
we confine our view to Anglo-Saxon institutions, there is less
difference between a "written" and a so-called "unwritten"
constitution than the terms "rigid" and "flexible," made current for them by Lord Bryce, would seem to imply. England
has had no such occasion, or rather no such necessity, as we in
America had about 1776, to codify her fundamental constitutional principles. But such principles did exist, and still do
exist, and in times of stress we hear occasional demands even
for a codification of them. From 1911 to 1914 the so-called
"die hards" or "last-ditchers" among the members of the House
of Lords were calling for some protection for themselves
stronger than their right of participation in all acts of parliament; and in 1914 a small group of unionists even proposed
the revival of the so-called royal veto on legislation in the case
of the Irish Home-Rule Bill, a branch of the royal prerogative
which had not been exercised for some two centuries.

In 1914 a short-lived review was founded to voice these
points of view, *The Candid Quarterly Review*. Its first number contains some remarkable statements whose gist may
probably be best gathered from an extract:

16

But the modern doctrine is that they [the former attributes of the King] have been somehow transferred from the King to the Minister; that they exist now only in the Minister. The Minister has become the King with all the Kingly attributes; the King has become the Minister with only the Ministerial duties. The gilt coach which bears the King to Parliament contains, in fact, Nothing: the taxicab which bears the Minister to Downing Street, Everything.[17]

This, the writer insists, is a great usurpation. The salaried parliament, the sale of honors, the Parliament Act of 1911, and the Irish Home-Rule Bill are all parts of a corrupt conspiracy to deprive the king of his prerogative and the people of their liberty. Therefore the king should exercise his legal and fundamental right, disused for two hundred years, and veto the Home-Rule Bill. The writer implies also that the Parliament Act, in leaving to the Lords a mere power of suspension, is void for unconstitutionality.

The Great War, which ensued in a few months, drew attention away from these constitutional questions, but they might come to the top again, and are almost sure to do so when a similar issue arises. It would, in short, not be surprising if in the years to come there were further, more frequent, and more widespread demands in England for "somewhat Fundamental, somewhat like a *Magna Charta*, that should be standing and be unalterable"—the words of Oliver Cromwell in 1654.[18] The extension of the elective franchise has been completed in England only in our own day. Most of it has occurred within the lifetime of men still living. And the political results of it are not yet fully apparent. The membership of the House of Commons, notwithstanding the successive enlargements of the electorate, is still to a great degree aristocratic, and aristocratic traditions still control and limit parliament's actions to an extent surprising to anyone who has not made a study of it. These traditions, inherited from an earlier time, still operate as inhibitions on parliamentary action almost as effective as legal prohibitions. So long as they do, the need for legal restrictions on the lawmaking organ will not be pressing, and the legal doctrine of the omnipotence of parliament is likely to remain little questioned. That doctrine is left unchallenged only because it has not yet been found to be dangerous to any class numerous enough and powerful enough successfully to oppose it.[19] On the other hand, it requires little prophetic insight to note that this situation cannot be permanent. The legal doctrine of parliament's omnipotence could never have persisted even to this day in England if its edge had not been blunted by conventions whose operation has been practically as invariable as that of the law itself.

When these conventions lose their effectiveness there will be a demand for law and the conventions will either be turned into laws or disregarded altogether. We have had an instance of this in recent times. Parliamentary omnipotence thus far has met its principal obstacle in imperial matters. The doctrine was challenged in North America in the eighteenth century and the American Revolution was the result. In our own time, in the recent Statute of Westminster, we have seen the breakdown of convention in Canada and the substitution of law in its place. It is natural that these striking instances of the growing inadequacy of convention should occur in the colonial sphere, where tradition is less firmly rooted than in the mother country. In England itself the equilibrium of law and convention has often been noted, especially since Walter Bagehot called attention to it in his classical analysis of the English constitution. Most persons are familiar with Bagehot's famous remarks on the prerogative, made in 1872 in the introduction to the second edition of his *English Constitution.* Without recourse to parliament, by an exercise of mere prerogative, the queen, he says,

could disband the army. . . . She could sell off all our ships of war and all our naval stores; she could make a peace by the sacrifice of Cornwall, and begin a war for the conquest of Brittany. She could make every citizen in the United Kingdom, male or female, a peer; she could make every parish in the United Kingdom a "university"; she could dismiss most of the civil servants: she could pardon all offenders.

What makes impossible the more serious of these prerogative rights Bagehot thought to be impeachment. But impeachment has long been obsolete, and was so in 1872 when Bagehot wrote. It seems very doubtful whether impeachment could be successfully revived for the conviction of a minister of state involved in such transactions. The possibility of revolution would seem to be the only real deterrent, just as it was in 1688 when James II made excessive use of a legitimate discretionary power. But in matters of this sort attention has in the past been directed mainly to the crown and the prerogative. The same threat of revolution effective against the crown, however, might be brought by the people against a parliament which outraged their feelings of what was just and right. This seems less likely to occur because parliament will in time come more and more to reflect the changing social and economic views of the new classes rising to political power. What we may expect for the near future, I think, is not a revolution against parliament but a transformation of it. Already, in the short period since the election of the first Labor representative, which some of us can remember, significant omens of change have appeared.

Anyone who frequented sessions of the House of Commons at the turn of the century and sees it now when some important and keenly contested social question is under discussion will be impressed by the difference. Outwardly there seems to be little change. The House of Commons looks just as it did and, when feelings are not aroused, it acts so too. But at times it is noticeable that language is less restrained than formerly in the House. Conventions inherited from the time when government and opposition were drawn from the same social class are broken more frequently. There is a subtle difference of atmosphere. When one considers the new elements that have entered parliament, it seems surprising that this change is no greater than it is, but a change has occurred nevertheless, and it is a symptom of possible changes to come much more fundamental in character. As the restraining influence of tradition grows weaker, the danger of a tyranny of the majority comes nearer, and the time may arrive when convention must give way to law if the rights of minorities are to be respected and safeguarded as they have been in the past. A popular despotism must result if the omnipotence of parliament ever becomes in practice what it now is in law. Because it is not yet so, England is today an exception more apparent than real to the principle laid down by Thomas Paine, that in any state in which the government constitutes itself "with what power it pleases" there is in reality "merely a form of government without a constitution."

As a general principle I think we must admit the truth of Paine's dictum that "a constitution is not the act of a government but of a people constituting a government." And, if this be true, the consequence is that the forms and limits followed in this "constituting" become the embodiment of a "constitution," superior in character to the acts of any "government" it creates. If, for example, this constituent act of the people entrusts certain definite powers to their government, "enumerated powers" as we term them, it is a necessary inference that this government cannot exercise any powers not so "enumerated." All constitutional government is by definition limited government. We may not agree that these limits are necessarily "antecedent" in the sense of that term that Paine had in mind, but for everyone they must be in some sense "fundamental," and fundamental not merely because they are basic, but because they are also unalterable by ordinary legal process.

The phase in the development of these political conceptions to which I have asked your attention thus far is the latest phase in that development, what might be called the "self-conscious" phase, in which the people are thought of as creating their constitution by direct and express constituent action. But I think enough has been shown to prove that this latest phase is only the outcome of an earlier and a much longer one, in which constitutions were thought of not as a creation but as a growth; not as a national code so much as a national inheritance. Our modern tendency to identify all law with legislation has modified the notions respecting constitutional as well as private law. We no longer think of either as the medieval man did, as custom, binding because it extends backward to a time "whereof the memory of man runneth not to the contrary."

It is the long development of this earlier and less conscious phase that I am to treat in more detail, but before doing so may I point out in advance what I hope will become obvious in the historical treatment, namely, that in all its successive phases, constitutionalism has one essential quality: it is a legal limitation on government; it is the antithesis of arbitrary rule; its opposite is despotic government, the government of will

21

instead of law. In modern times the growth of political responsibility has been added to this through the winning of the initiative in the discretionary matters of national policy by the people's representatives, and of that more anon; but the most ancient, the most persistent, and the most lasting of the essentials of true constitutionalism still remains what it has been almost from the beginning, the limitation of government by law. "Constitutional limitations," if not the most important part of our constitutionalism, are beyond doubt the most ancient.

CHAPTER II

The Ancient Conception
of a Constitution

IN THE *Oxford Dictionary*, which I have long thought of as the best single textbook of the history of our peculiar institutions and ideas, several meanings of the word "constitution" are listed. It may mean the act of establishing or of ordaining, or the ordinance or regulation so established. It may mean the "make" or composition which determines the nature of anything, and may thus be applied to the body or the mind of man as well as to external objects. In the Roman Empire the word in its Latin form became the technical term for acts of legislation by the emperor, and from Roman law the Church borrowed it and applied it to ecclesiastical regulations for the whole Church or for some particular ecclesiastical province. From the Church, or possibly from the Roman lawbooks themselves, the term came back into use in the later middle ages as applicable to secular enactments of the time. In England the famous Constitutions of Clarendon of 1164 were referred to by Henry II and others as "constitutions," *avitae constitutiones* or *leges,* a *recordatio vel recognitio* of the relations purporting to have existed between church and state in the time of Henry's grandfather, Henry I. But in substance these were ecclesiastical provisions even though they were promulgated by secular authority, and this may account for the application to them of the word "constitutions." The word, however, is often found in a purely secular use at this time; though scarcely in any technical sense, for we find other words such as *lex* or *edictum* used interchangeably with *constitutio* for a secular administrative enactment.[1] As just noted, the Constitutions of Clarendon are referred to in the document itself as a "record" (*recordatio*) or a "finding" (*recognitio*). The author of the *Leges Henrici Primi,* who wrote early in the twelfth century, soon after the appearance of Henry I's well-known writ for the holding of the hundred and county courts, also refers to that writ as a "record."[2] Glanvill frequently uses the word "constitution" for a royal edict. He refers to Henry II's writ creating the remedy by grand assize as *legalis ista constitutio,*[3] and calls the assize of novel disseisin both a *recognitio* and a *constitutio.*[4] Bracton, writing a few years after the statute of Merton of 1236, calls one of its provisions a "new constitution,"[5] and refers to a section of Magna Carta reissued in 1225 as *constitutio libertatis.*[6] In France about the same time Beaumanoir speaks of the remedy in novel disseisin as *une nouvele constitucion* made by the kings.[7]

At this time, and for centuries after, "constitution" always means a particular administrative enactment much as it had meant to the Roman lawyers. The word is used to distinguish such particular enactments from *consuetudo* or ancient custom. It is apparently never used in our modern sense, to denote the whole legal framework of the state. It would require a very detailed examination of the legal and political writings of several centuries to enable one to say with any confidence when this modern notion of a constitution first appears. I cannot claim to have made any such examination, but I cannot recall from my reading any clear instance of it before the opening of the seventeenth century. In 1578 Pierre Grégoire of Toulouse uses the word almost in our modern sense in his

24

De Republica, but the context seems to me to indicate a somewhat wider and more general sense of *constitutio* than the strictly political meaning the word "constitution" now conveys, for which Grégoire seems to use the older phrase *status reipublicae.*[8] The first instance given in the *Oxford Dictionary* of the use of the word "constitution" for the whole legal framework of a state is a phrase of Bishop Hall's in 1610, "The Constitution of the Common-wealth of Israel," and in my first lecture I quoted some words of Sir James Whitelocke's of the same year, possibly not quite so definite but even more striking: "the natural frame and constitution of the policy of this Kingdom, which is *jus publicum regni.*"

This use of the term "constitution" may have been new in 1610, but the idea it conveys is in reality one of the oldest, if not the very oldest, in the whole history of constitutionalism. Whitelocke's phrase which I have just given—"the natural frame and constitution of the policy [i.e., polity] of this Kingdom, which is *jus publicum regni*"—in reality includes two conceptions of a constitution closely connected and at times combined, but nevertheless distinct in character. One appears in Whitelocke's first words, "the natural frame of the state," and this idea seems as old as the *politeia* of the Greeks, which we usually translate by our word "constitution." The other conception is expressed by Whitelocke's other phrase, *"jus publicum regni,"* the public law of the realm. The latter conception may not be as ancient as the former, but it is very old. Cicero, for example, voices it in his *De Re Publica* in a passage which contains the first use that I know of the word "constitution" in its accepted modern sense. In commending a mixed form of government, Cicero says, "This constitution (*haec constitutio*) has a great measure of equability without which men can hardly remain free for any length of time." [9] Further on he says,

"Now that opinion of Cato becomes more certain, that the constitution of the republic (*constitutionem rei publicae*) is the work of no single time or of no single man." [10]

It is these two forms of early constitutionalism expressed by the Greek *politeia* and by the Latin *constitutio*, and their inter-relations in history, that I propose to try to trace; and I shall begin with the more ancient, the *politeia* of the Greeks.

Of all the varied meanings of which our word "constitution" is susceptible, the Greek *politeia* conforms to one of the most ancient. It means above all the state as it actually is. It is a term which comprises all the innumerable characteristics which determine that state's peculiar nature, and these include its whole economic and social texture as well as matters governmental in our narrower modern sense. It is a purely descriptive term, and as inclusive in its meaning as our own use of the word "constitution" when we speak generally of a man's constitution or of the constitution of matter. As Sir Paul Vinogradoff says:

The Greeks recognized a close analogy between the organization of the State and the organism of the individual human being. They thought that the two elements of body and mind, the former guided and governed by the latter, had a parallel in two constitutive elements of the State, the rulers and the ruled. [11]

There is nothing in the Greek language "corresponding to the Latin *jus*." [12] It is

characteristic of the development of Greek juridical ideas that the "law of nature," though appealed to as a philosophical explanation of existing facts, does not serve as a means for concrete juridical deductions. It was at a later stage—with the advent of Stoicism, especially in its Roman form—that the law of nature began to be

26

considered as a source of law in the practical sense of the term.[13]

In Athens there was no consolidated constitution.[14]

The analogy between state organization and the human organism involved, as Mr. W. L. Newman truly says,

that which was to a Greek the central inquiry of Political Science. . . . It was thus that in the view of the Greeks every constitution had an accompanying ἦθος, which made itself felt in all the relations of life. Each constitutional form exercised a moulding influence on virtue; the good citizen was a different being in an oligarchy, a democracy, and an aristocracy. Each constitution embodied a scheme of life, and tended, consciously or not, to bring the lives of those living under it into harmony with its particular scheme. If the law provides that the highest offices in the State shall be purchasable or confines them to wealthy men, it inspires *ipso facto* a respect for wealth in the citizens.[15]

From the Greek political classics instances almost without number might be given of this conception of a constitution as the ἦθος of a people, but I can mention only one or two. "Our whole state," Plato says in the *Laws*, "is an 'imitation' (μίμησις) of the best and noblest life." [16] In the *Panathenaicus* Isocrates says that the *politeia* is the "soul (ψυχή) of the *polis*" with power over it like that of the mind over the body; [17] and Aristotle, in the *Politics*, calls it "in a sense the life of the city." [18] From this conception of the nature of the constitution, in which Greeks of every philosophical party seemed to share, there followed results of great importance both theoretical and practical.

As Sir Paul Vinogradoff says, there is nothing in the Greek language which quite corresponds to the Latin word *jus;* and there seems to be nothing in the Greek conception of the state or of its constitution to correspond to the *jus regni* of Sir James

27

Whitelocke. The Greeks made no such clear distinction as the Roman one between *jus publicum* and *jus privatum;* their politics consisted of a philosophical explanation of actual facts rather than a basis for concrete juridical deductions. Natural law, if admitted at all, became the criterion merely of the comparative excellence of a state's form of government; it never became for the Greeks as for the Romans the test of a government's legitimacy. And by the Sophists of every kind natural law was not admitted at all. "The tribe of Sophists," as Plato says in his *Sophista,* "is not easily caught or defined"; but the subjectivism or relativity that marked the philosophy of them all precluded even a comparison of constitutions, because it denied the existence of any values, or norms, or objective standards, which alone could warrant anyone in saying that one state's constitution was better or worse than another's. And even the great opponents of the Sophists, such as Plato and Aristotle, in their assertion of objective reality and of the possibility of man's apprehending it, although they believed in a universal law of nature, never went so far as to say that this was a coercive law. They never could have said as Cicero did, that states have no power through senate or people to free themselves from it.[19] Natural law meant to them, as to the modern scientist, no more than the *fact* of invariability. It carried with it no notion of sanction.

One of the clearest statements of this Greek attitude toward the fundamental relations of government to law is to be found in the *Politicus* or *Statesman* of Plato, a dialogue whose central theme is the problem of "constitutionalism"—of all Plato's dialogues the one most directly concerned with the subject we have now in hand. I have long felt that this dialogue, though less fundamental, no doubt, than the *Republic,* has been too much neglected in our estimate of Plato's real political position and purpose; and not of his own position alone, but of the normal attitude toward constitutionalism in the Academy and the Lyceum at least, if not in Greece generally.

It was mainly with this work, rather than with the *Republic*, Professor Jaeger insists, that Aristotle's study of Plato's political doctrines was concerned,[20] and he shows conclusively throughout his remarkable book how vitally important that study was in forming the political conception which Aristotle held to the very end. "He had accepted Plato's doctrines with his whole soul," Professor Jaeger says, "and the effort to discover his own relation to them occupied all his life, and is the clue to his development." [21]

The central question discussed in the *Politicus* is the perennial one of the proper relation of government to law. Plato has been claimed as a fellow by some of the modern proponents of the totalitarian state, but how anyone could honestly make such a claim after he had carefully pondered the *Politicus* is wholly beyond my comprehension. If one should disregard Plato's plain statements of his purpose in the *Republic*, it is perhaps conceivable that one might distort that dialogue into a defense of actual arbitrary governments; yet the whole discussion in the *Politicus* plainly shows that this is not Plato's true position but the very antithesis of it.

It is true that even in the *Politicus* the defects of constitutional governments are clearly recognized. In fact they are probably stated with greater distinctness in this dialogue than in any other of the Platonic writings. Constitutional government, Plato admits, is to be regarded only as a "second best" (ὡς δεύτερον as compared with τὸ πρῶτον). But the "first" or best type of political relations, a government unhampered by law, is, he declares unequivocally, only an ideal of which actual states can never be more than an approximation, and usually

29

not a very close approximation. Limitations of law always do hamper government; and, provided the government is a good one, there may be good things that such a government can achieve, if unrestricted, which these limitations of law render impossible of accomplishment.

The problem that Plato faces here is a practical one that is likely to persist as long as government itself. A constitutional government will always be a weak government when compared with an arbitrary one. There will be many desirable things, as well as undesirable, which are easy for a despotism but impossible elsewhere. Constitutionalism suffers from the defects inherent in its own merits. Because it cannot do some evil it is precluded from doing some good. Shall we, then, forego the good to prevent the evil, or shall we submit to the evil to secure the good? This is the fundamental practical question of all constitutionalism. It is the foremost issue in the present political world; and it is amazing, and to many of us very alarming, to consider to what insufferable barbarities nation after nation today is showing a willingness to submit, for the recompense it thinks it is getting or hopes to get from an arbitrary government. This great problem is the central one in Plato's dialogue, and Plato's answer to it cannot but interest the present-day reformer as well as the historian of constitutional development.

That answer is based on the fundamental distinction, but at the same time the very close connection, sometimes overlooked or underestimated, between the ideal on the one hand and the actual or the attainable. Plato's *Republic* deals with an unattainable ideal; his *Politicus* treats of the attainable in its relation to this same ideal. The attainable is less perfect than the ideal, and it is the presence of legal restriction that makes it so; for law, as Plato says, is like an obstinate and ignorant tyrant who will not allow anything to be done contrary to his appointment or any question to be asked —not even in sudden changes of circumstances, when something happens to be better than what he commanded for some one.

The law cannot comprehend exactly what is noblest or more just, or at once ordain what is best, for all. The differences of men and actions, and the endless irregular movements of human things, do not admit of any universal and simple rule. No art can lay down any rule which will last forever.

A perfectly simple principle can never be applied to a state of things which is the reverse of simple.

How familiar these objections to constitutionalism sound! Their burden is always the present insufficiency of law inherited from some "horse and buggy" era in the past. And of course no one could deny the validity of such objections. There is a practical recognition of them in the history of our equitable remedies for the deficiencies of rigid legal rules, and the entrusting to governments of a discretionary power in exceptional cases to dispense with law or to pardon a breach of it necessarily implies the admission that this law, especially if it is an ancient law, can never secure adequate justice in every particular case. The principal defect of all law is at the same time its most essential and most valuable characteristic—its generality.

It was considerations such as these that led Plato to hold that the best government theoretically or ideally is one based upon the discretion of the ruler and not upon law; and such a government conforms precisely to the meaning of our word "despotism"—in this case a perfectly benevolent despotism, of course. So he asks:

31

As the pilot watches over the interests of the ship, or of the crew, and preserves the lives of his fellow sailors, not by laying down rules, *but by making his art a law*—even so, and in the self-same way, may there not be a true form of polity created by those who are able to govern in a similar spirit, and who show a *strength of art which is superior to the law?* [22]

From this sentence it is evident, as it is from the whole tenor of the dialogue, that the ideally best rule exists where the ruler is not limited by law but makes *his art a law*. But another thing is equally evident here and equally prominent throughout the *Politicus,* namely, that this "art" of the ruler shows "a strength of art which is *superior* to the law." This brings up the final and most crucial question of all. Is Plato in this dialogue insisting on the superiority of despotism over constitutionalism as a principle of practical politics, or is he trying to illustrate the very opposite? To put it more concretely, does Plato believe in the actual or possible existence of any ruler with such "strength of art" that his "art" should be the only law of the state? He evidently believes such a philosopher-king ought to rule as a despot if you could only find him. But does he believe that such an incomparable embodiment of omniscience, omnicompetence, and utter benevolence could possibly exist except in the imagination? It is interesting to note the historical tendency of peoples generally to deify their rulers once they have conceded despotic authority to them. A divine competence in a ruler is in fact the only real justification of a despotism; and where there is despotism the apotheosis of the ruler is likely sooner or later to appear in some form. It is interesting but not strange to find Cardinal Ballarmine in the sixteenth century arguing that the Church should have a despotic government because the Church is divine, while the state ought to have a limited government because the state is human. The answer to the question whether Plato was politically an absolutist or a constitutionalist depends then on the answer to another: Did Plato believe that his philosopher-king had appeared or could possibly appear in any actual state on earth? Through what seems to me a misinterpretation of the *Republic,* some have attributed the latter view to Plato, but the whole argument of the *Politicus* is against it; and I cannot agree with those who find in the *Politicus* inconsistency with the *Republic* or a contradiction of it. Like Cardinal Ballarmine, and on much the same general grounds, Plato regarded absolute government as the only celestial one and celestial government as the only one properly absolute.

A godlike ruler should rule like a god, and if a godlike man should appear among men, godlike rule would and should be gladly conceded to him. This was Aristotle's view, and he may well have got it from the teachings of Plato. But I know of nothing in all Plato's writings which indicates a belief in the actual, or even the possible, existence of a superman like this; and without such a demigod despotism becomes for Plato, not the best, but the worst of all possible governments. Between these two extremes lay his second-best state under constitutional rule. It is of little consequence that there should be one ruler, or a few or many rulers, in such a state, provided the government be limited by law; and, in the cases where it is so limited, Plato finds an approximation of the "art" of the perfect despot close enough to warrant him in speaking of monarchy, aristocracy, and a constitutional democracy as forms of government, sadly defective indeed, but true; in comparison with the three corresponding perverted forms, in all of which men totally devoid of any "strength of art" superior to the law— the only justification of despotism—have nevertheless made their own art the state's sole law.

It may seem a paradox, if not even worse, to say, as Plato does here, that actual despotisms are less closely akin to the ideal despotism than these constitutional governments which at first sight seem so much less like it. But to Plato it is not the external form of a state that differentiates it from another, but the guiding inner principle of its political life, above all the presence or absence of justice. In a constitutional government the laws under which the state is ruled are far inferior to the wisdom of the perfect ruler, chiefly on account of their rigidity; but these laws are none the less "imitations" ($\mu\iota\mu\acute{\eta}\mu\alpha\tau\alpha$) of that perfect wisdom—very faulty "copies" of the government of the ideal state. They *are* copies, and copies which to Plato embody a greater measure of true justice than the arbitrary will of vicious or ignorant men can ever do; and even the best of men are more or less vicious and ignorant. Law, as Aristotle says, is "intelligence without passion." [23]

For the subject with which we are immediately concerned—constitutionality in its actual rather than its ideal form—the *Politicus* seems to disclose Plato's real opinions more clearly than his description of omniscient despotism in the unattainable ideal of the *Republic*. If the *Politicus* gives us a true picture of its author's mind, he was certainly no advocate of arbitrary government in the actual political world. In this dialogue he does not explain at length just why he thinks national custom a safer guide than the fiat of government, but he gives unmistakable evidence that he does think so. His preference for the *Rechtsstaat* may have been mainly pragmatic. In the *Laws* he notes that all other states are "on the highway to ruin," [24] and appeals to that right reason "which the law affirms, and which the experience of the best of our elders has agreed to be truly right." [25] But whatever the grounds for it may have been, his belief in the superiority of law over will

34

as a principle of actual government can hardly be doubted.

If then the *Politicus* gives a true indication of Plato's political beliefs, and if my hurried summary of it is not inaccurate, there is little comfort to be derived from him by believers in totalitarianism.

One further point alone I can stop to note about his constitutionalism. In common with Socrates and Aristotle and in opposition to the Sophists, he believed in a universal norm of political life to be apprehended through human reason or "nature," by which the various forms of polity may be judged and compared; and this norm might be roughly termed a "law of nature." But there is one striking difference between the conception of a "law of nature" as he held it—and as did apparently all his Greek contemporaries of every party—and the one later transmitted by the Stoics to Rome. The law of nature is to him no more than a basis of comparison. He thinks of this law, as he thinks of all law, merely as an intellectual standard. Law is nothing more than the uniformity of nature, and human law is likewise nothing but the common apprehension of a part of this uniformity by man. It is thus a common "yardstick" by which one form of polity may be compared on its merits with another, and even one enactment made within a state with another. The latter is the distinction between true law in the abstract (νόμος) and particular laws (νομιζόμενα), dealt with in the Platonic dialogue *Minos*—Platonic whether by Plato or not. Such particular laws are good when they embody the true law and not otherwise.

But with this comparison of polities or of laws Greek constitutionalism of the classical period seems to stop. It goes no further than mere intellectual assessment or comparison. It may pronounce that a given polity or particular law is bad; it does not go on to say it is not binding. It may even say that these bad enactments are not true law at all, but it does not say they can be disregarded. As Rehm observes, the customary definition of the state was not a legal definition at all, but a political one; [26] the ancient theorists were concerned primarily with an "ethico-political appraisal of the relations between the state and other forms of human association," [27] not with the "sovereignty" which bulks so large in all modern discussions of political relations. Aristotle's word for the supremacy in a state corresponding to our "sovereignty," τὸ κύριον, does not imply supreme constituted authority, as sovereignty does, but a supremacy in fact only.[28] In short, the conception of constitutionalism based on the notion of law prevailing generally in this period is of a constitution in the primitive sense noted above, of the whole nature or "composure" of a thing. Such a conception of law may warrant one in saying that a particular enactment is bad, but never that it is not legitimate. There is no room under such a conception for any distinction such as we make between a provision that is binding because constitutional and one that is void for unconstitutionality. What this amounts to is that "the law of the constitution," if we might employ such a phrase, is not coercive but only normative; and that constitutions have no sanction in our modern sense. Whatever the phrase "an unconstitutional law" might have meant for Plato or for Aristotle, if he had ever used it, it would never have meant a law void on account of unconstitutionality; and, while a "constitutional law" might conceivably have meant one concerned with the framework of the state, it could never have been a "fundamental" law in our sense of that phrase.

The difference just noted between our notion of constitutionality and the antique one is only one aspect of the difference between the modern and the ancient view of the state in general. Before the Stoics, Greeks apparently drew no clear distinction between society and the state, between the social and the civil. But institutions that are thus identical must also be coeval. Potentially at least, the state must therefore be as old as human association, there is no science of society apart from politics, and there can be no natural law older than the laws of actual states. As a consequence, the Greeks thought of the law in a state only as one part or rather as one aspect of the whole polity itself, never as something outside or apart from the state to which that polity must conform, nor even as any special provision within the state to which other laws are subordinate. If the Greeks thought of a law of nature as applying to a particular state at all, they meant by this natural law no more than that portion of a state's actual laws which *in fact* happens to be identical in all other states—what Aristotle in his *Rhetoric* called "common law" (κοινὸς νόμος); [29] they had in mind no "fundamental" principles which must invalidate a municipal law inconsistent with them; in short, they thought of law in terms of the state, not of the state in terms of law, as the Roman and the medieval man invariably did. It was only after the appearance of a notion of a higher and an *older* law, out of which the laws of particular states are fashioned and to which they must conform in order to be valid, that the modern conception of constitutionalism could replace the ancient one. The change, however, has come when Cicero can define a state as a bond of law (*vinculum juris*); for here by law he means no law of the state itself, but an antecedent law, and one antecedent in time as well as sanction. He says expressly in his *De Re Publica* that this law is as old as the mind of God, existing long before there were any states in the world. But more important still, he adds that no state can ever enact any binding law in derogation of this law of nature, a statement that no Greek of the fifth or fourth century B.C. could have dreamt of making, even supposing that he could have understood it.

There is probably no change in the whole history of political theory more revolutionary than this, and certainly none so momentous for the future of constitutionalism. From this great difference between the ancient and the modern conception of constitutionalism some very important practical results may be traced. Since, under the older conception, the *politeia,* or constitution as we may call it, included not merely a *jus publicum regni* but the whole life of the state, two or three great practical differences between ancient and modern states seem to be logically incident to it, differences that even a slight comparison of ancient and modern constitutional history clearly discloses. First, in the ancient regime there is no remedy for an unconstitutional act short of actual revolution. Secondly, such revolution, when it occurs, is usually no mere modification of the "public law," such as Whitelocke's *jus publicum regni,* but a complete overturn of the state's institutions, a change in its whole way of life. It is a social as well as a merely "political" revolution in our modern narrower sense of "political." Aristotle refers to such revolutions as a dissolution of the polities in which they occur; the "constitutions" and with them the states themselves are destroyed, or rather, actually "dissolved" (λύονται).[30] Thirdly, it is this fundamental and far-reaching character of most actual revolutions in Greece, in so many cases touching everything in the state, social, economic, and intellectual, as well as governmental; changes usually carried out by violence, proscription, ostracism, and even death, in ways very similar to the proceedings so familiar to us in parts of Europe today and with much the same underlying causes—it is this wholesale character of so many contemporary revolutions that accounts for the Greek fear of *stasis,* and the nervous desire to risk almost anything that might prevent it. For *stasis* is a lack of equilibrium, a condition of disharmony in a state, which is almost sure to entail unrest and eventual revolution with all its usual horrors. Nothing less than such revolution and the constant dread of its results could have led Aristotle, for example, to advise tyrants how to prolong a type of government which he admits to be the most oppressive in the world as well as the shortest-lived; and Aristotle's attitude toward *stasis* indicated in the *Politics* is reflected in most of the political writings surviving from Aristotle's time in Greece. The Greek states were notoriously unstable, and this situation led to a desire to preserve the *status quo* which to us seems at times almost reactionary. The analysis that Aristotle gives of the causes of sedition is as keen as the remedies are often cynical. One has to pinch himself to realize that he is not reading from some résumé of recent events in Europe when, for example, Aristotle says:

It is as little possible to create a state in any arbitrary period of time as to create it of any arbitrary population. Accordingly the great majority of states to which a number of alien colonists have been admitted at the time of their foundation, or at a later date, have been the scenes of violent sedition.[31]

Or this:

Polities generally are liable to dissolution not only from within but from without, when there is a state having an antagonistic polity near to them or distant but possessed of considerable power.[32]

Or take the following summary he gives of the measures usually adopted and actually necessary to preserve a tyranny:

The practice of cutting off prominent characters and putting out of the way the high spirits in the state; the prohibition of common meals, political clubs, high culture and everything else of the same kind; precautionary measures against all that tends to produce two results, *viz.*, spirit and confidence; the opposition offered to literary *réunions* or any other meetings of a literary kind, and the endeavor by every possible means to produce the greatest mutual ignorance among all the citizens, as it is acquaintance that tends to produce mutual confidence.[33]

"Another expedient," he says,

is the endeavor to prevent any word or action of any subject from escaping detection by a system of spies. . . . For the citizens are then less free of speech for fear of the spies and, if they do speak freely, are more easily discovered.[34]

And, he adds,

A tyrant is fond of making wars, as a means of keeping his subjects in employment and in continual need of a commander.[35]

The sum of all such measures, Aristotle concludes, is "to prevent mutual confidence among the citizens, to incapacitate them for action, and to degrade their spirit." [36]

From these notions of constitutionalism prevailing in ancient Greece which I have been trying to summarize, we must proceed next to the character of the changes which made such notions so radically different when we first meet them among the Romans some three centuries later; and this change in constitutionalism seems to be bound up with a change in the definition of natural law, which must be briefly indicated before the beginnings of Roman or medieval constitutionalism themselves can be made clear.

The Constitutionalism of Rome and Its Influence

THE OFTENER I survey the whole history of constitutionalism the more I am impressed with the significance and importance of the republican constitution of Rome in that development. A generation or two ago it was the fashion to trace all
our constitutional liberties back to the institutions of the
Germanic tribes as described by Tacitus. Rome had contributed little or nothing to medieval or modern institutions or
ideas in this field beyond the absolutist maxim of the Empire
that "what has pleased the prince has the force of an enactment of the people." Modern absolutism was a return to
Roman autocracy; liberty was solely a retention in the face of
it of the freedom of the primitive Germanic peoples. It was
sometimes overlooked that Tacitus himself, when he contrasted the virtues of primitive Germany with the degeneracy
of Rome, had written with Roman imperial institutions in
mind, not those of the Republic. There was undoubted truth
in this Germanic interpretation, but its exaggeration had been
undermined by more careful historical research long before
the recent deplorable exhibitions of tribalism in Germany.
Even before these startling modern developments some of us
had begun to question some of the conclusions of the German
oracle, Otto von Gierke, in his *Genossenschaftsrecht*. The reaction of the Germanists against the more extreme defenders

41

of *Pandektenrecht* such as Bernhard Windscheid, and the substitution of a more Germanic code of law in place of the original draft at the opening of this century are easy enough to understand and may have been both necessary and beneficial; but the recent appalling effects of tribal particularism have served to heighten the suspicion held by some of us a good while before, that after all the impressive apparatus of Gierke's *Genossenschaftsrecht* sometimes merely conceals the weakness of some of its principal historical conclusions instead of really strengthening them. The too ready acceptance of these conclusions by F. W. Maitland, the greatest of all our modern historians of English medieval institutions, unfortunately created a vogue in England and America for these views which a careful examination of them seems hardly to justify.

In returning to our subject proper, the institutions of Rome under the Republic, I shall try to avoid as far as possible the thorny question of origins. Cicero is the first expositor of these institutions whose works are known in any great detail, and Cicero was at once a practicing lawyer and a pupil and paraphraser of Panaetius. Is it the Roman lawyer then who is speaking, or the Hellenistic Stoic, when Cicero sets forth in his *De Re Publica* and his *De Legibus* the fundamental relations of the state to law? It is a question I am not competent to answer nor even to try to answer. I shall confine myself therefore to the general principles of the Roman constitution as it actually was in the last century or two of the Republic, or rather so far as we can safely reconstruct it from the surviving contemporary materials. Even in the realm of the actual, it may seem strange to some that I should pay such slight attention to those checks and balances so admired by Polybius and Machiavelli and so despised by Mommsen. My excuse is that these balances, while possibly the most original of Rome's permanent contributions to constitutionalism, are very far indeed from being the most important then, or the most significant now.

We cannot hope to bridge the gap between the constitutionalism of Aristotle and that of Cicero, but even the most superficial comparison of the two will show that a gap is there, and a very wide one. As Dr. Carlyle says:

There is no change in political theory so startling in its completeness as the change from the theory of Aristotle to the later philosophical view represented by Cicero and Seneca. . . . We have ventured to suggest that the dividing-line between the ancient and the modern political theory must be sought, if anywhere, in the period between Aristotle and Cicero.[1]

What is true of political is usually true also of constitutional theory; the two are often nearly indistinguishable, and never more nearly so than in Rome. We should in all probability have to look back as far as republican Rome for the beginnings of our "modern" theory, constitutional as well as political; and we could probably look back little if any further than republican Rome with any assurance.

For the distinctive general principles of Roman constitutionalism under the later Republic—the general principles, the "spirit," rather than the minute details, the thing most important for us here—I have never found any modern guide more suggestive or more penetrating than Rudolf von Ihering's monumental *Geist des römischen Rechts*. The author's universalism—a universalism which implies an essential individualism—is shown in his assertion that peoples formed by a mingling of races are usually distinguished by their persistent energy, a marked characteristic of the Romans and in modern times of the English, who most resemble them.

43

But the Roman characteristic of greatest significance for constitutional history is reflected in the fact that we have to wait so long to find in any legal writer the plain statement that a ruler's will actually is law. It is clear, say the authors of Justinian's *Institutes,* quoting Ulpian, that a command of the emperor in due form is a *lex:* "Quodcumque igitur imperator per epistulam constituit vel cognoscens decrevit, vel edicto praecepit, *legem esse constat.*" All these expressions of the emperor's will actually are *leges,* and apparently no predecessor earlier than Ulpian had ever ventured to say so much. The most Gaius will say, even in the second century after Christ, is that it has never been doubted that the will of the Emperor duly expressed should receive the obedience owing to a *lex.* It is not itself a *lex.* Gaius does not even quite say, as the authors of Justinian's *Institutes* do, though I think he does mean to imply, that it has the full·force of a *lex* (*legis habet vigorem*); his express words are that there is no doubt that any imperial constitution, like a *senatus consultum,* should have the place of a *lex* (*legis vicem optineat*). And for this he gives one reason and one alone—"because the Emperor himself receives his *imperium* by virtue of a *lex* (*per legem*)." [2]

It is clear that the key to the source of all political authority at Rome is the definition of a *lex.* A *lex,* Gaius says in the second century, "is what the people orders and has established." Some four centuries later Justinian's *Institutes* define it as "what the Roman people was accustomed to establish when initiated by a senatorial magistrate such as a consul." In the exhaustive list of the various kinds of Roman legal enactment which Gaius gives—he has nothing whatever to say concerning the authority of unwritten law or custom—*lex* stands first, the enactment of the whole people; while the authority of every other form of Roman legislation invariably depends upon its relation to *lex*. Thus the patricians, we are told, had refused to be bound by enactments made by the plebs alone till these were "equated" with *leges* by a *lex* passed by the whole *populus* itself. Decrees of the Senate were never *leges*, but in time came to be accepted in place of *lex* (*legis vicem optinet*); though Gaius hints at existing doubts of their validity, which probably resulted from the non existence for decrees of the Senate of any particular *lex* similar to the *Lex Hortensia* by which plebiscites had been made equivalent to *leges*. Notwithstanding such doubts, as the *Institutes* of Justinian somewhat vaguely say, in the course of time "it seemed just (*aequum*) that the Senate should be consulted" in place of the *populus*, because the latter had become too great in number to meet for purposes of legislation. It might be said that observance of the Senate's decrees always depended on a "convention of the constitution" rather than a law. As Cicero put it in his *De Legibus, "potestas in populo, auctoritas in senatu."* [3] It was the very necessity of the case, as Pomponius says in an extract preserved in Justinian's *Digest,* that imposed on the Senate the care of the Republic.[4] The distinction implied by the letters SPQR, *Senatus Populusque Romanus,* on the Roman standards really meant something. The constitutional difference and the interrelation of senate and *populus* were roughly analogous to those existing between a modern English "government" and an English parliament.

Constitutions of the Emperor also, like decrees of the Senate, had for Gaius the effect of *lex* without themselves becoming *leges;* but, on the other hand, by the second century after Christ none could possibly doubt the full legal equivalence of an imperial constitution with a *lex,* as he might of a *senatus consultum;* for the Emperor by a definite *lex* had received his *imperium*—nothing less than the *whole* of (*omne*) the peo-

45

ple's *imperium* and *potestas,* as Justinian's *Institutes* later
phrase it—and more than one of these regal laws were in
existence.[5]

Whatever the fact, of the theory of the Roman constitution
we can have no doubt: the people, and the people alone, are
the source of all law. As Rehm says, "The assembly of the people is the state; not merely the organ of the *populus,* but the
populus itself." [6] SPQR means senate and *populus,* not senate
and any assembly even roughly representing the people.

For an understanding of the essential spirit of Roman constitutionalism, above all other things, a consideration of the
nature of *lex* is necessary.

"It may be said that the Romans have fixed for all time the
categories of juristic thought," says one of the ablest modern
historians of the Roman law; [7] and undoubtedly one of their
greatest permanent contributions to constitutionalism was the
distinction they made, more clearly than it had been made
before, or was to be made for long afterward, between the
jus publicum and the *jus privatum*—a distinction that lies to
this day behind the whole history of our legal safeguards of the
rights of the individual against encroachment of government.
But the true nature of this important distinction is likely to be
lost if we forget the close relation that also existed between
the private law of Rome and the public. Both were *jus,* and the
same spirit animated them. Public law, as the authors of Justinian's *Institutes* say, is only that part of *jus "quod ad statum
rei Romanae spectat";* private law is "that which pertains to
the utility of individuals." Their essence is the same; their difference lies in their incidence rather than their nature. As
Ihering says in a remarkable passage: [8] The state, as a bearer
of rights, is the whole of the citizens, the *civitas;* it is no ab-
straction apart from the people, and therefore these rights in-

46

here in the people themselves, and what is more, in each of them individually. Public and private rights are not distinguishable in having what the Germans call "subjects" different from each other. The "subject" is always exactly the same for both, the natural person. The sole difference between them lies in the fact that private rights affect private individuals exclusively, while all the individual citizens alike participate in the public. A concrete proof of the correctness of this contention is to be found in the Roman *actio popularis,* which was open to any private citizen in case of an infringement of the common rights of all.

And what was thus true of rights was equally true of duties, as appears in the fact that a Roman citizen who violated a treaty with another nation was surrendered to the other nation "because he had broken an obligation which rested on him personally." [9]

It is then an inversion of the true historical order to infer, as some have done, that the principles of Roman private law were merely those drawn from the public. The general principles were the same in both, but their earliest application is to be seen far more clearly in relations between individual citizens than in the field of constitutional law proper. The primary notion in each is the independence of the individual, and, as Ihering says again, it was only after a long and bitter struggle that the dominance of the state over him was finally established.

The most effective safeguard of the rights of individual against individual was ultimately found in the guarantee of the people to protect these rights. The observance of the terms of a will, for example, was secured by "registering" it, as we should say, in the *comitia calata;* and similar instances of private transactions thus publicly guaranteed are numerous in

47

the early law, such as *mancipatio, nexum,* and the like. The whole people became "responsible" for the maintenance of the individual rights thus created by private act or agreement. These were very concrete rights in the beginning, and the later refined notion that the state is the protector of right in the abstract is the outcome of a long development. In legal history, not only in Rome but elsewhere, the truth of Sir Henry Maine's famous generalization is obvious. In the beginning the principles of the law are "gradually secreted in the interstices of procedure," [10] and the development of that procedure itself is tentative, from one particular remedy to another, as needs gradually require. The true historical order has been the converse of the logical: principles have developed slowly as a rationalization of existing and only partial remedies; remedies have not been means devised to enforce principles antecedent.

Early legal development is everywhere the gradual merging of *damna absque injuria*—wrongs without a legal remedy—in a growing list of actionable injuries; and in the beginning the *damna* were far more numerous than the *injuriae*. As Maitland puts it for England in his incomparable way, "writs, not rights," must be the subject of any study of the early history of law.

It is only from such a study that we can get a notion of the true content of the word *lex* in Roman constitutional development, and I should like to add to *lex* one other word of almost equal significance, not only for Roman constitutional ideas themselves, but for the later influence of these ideas as well—the word *sponsio*.

Lex in its fully developed constitutional sense is a form of obligation applicable to the people as a whole, but if one were to look through the extracts preserved in the *Digest* for instances of the use of the word, he would be struck by the many cases in which it clearly refers merely to obligations subsisting between individual citizens. I can give but few of the many instances. Here is one extract from the *Responses* of Scaevola:

A controversy has arisen between an heir at law and an heir under a will and has been terminated after an arrangement by a definite agreement (*certa lege*). I ask which one creditors can sue.[11]

Another, from the *Quaestiones* of Paulus, is as follows:

It has been asked whether any action lies if a son has been given you by adoption with this proviso (*hac lege*), that after say three years you should give him to me by adoption. And Labeo thought there was no action.[12]

The last of these dry quotations—and it must be the last—is from Ulpian's commentary on the Edict:

If in the course of an action of wardship it is agreed that interest shall be paid beyond the legal rate, this shall have no effect, for this would ground an action on the agreement; whereas those terms are essential which determine the conditions of the contract (*quae legem contractui dant*); namely, those entered into when it was made.[13]

Gaius uses *lex* in the same sense when he speaks of a lease of lands with this stipulation (*ea lege*), that the heirs of the lessee shall remain in possession,[14] and refers to the hiring of a band of gladiators with a condition (*ea lege*) respecting those who shall be killed or injured.[15] A *lex* was a contract between private individuals. But, as we have seen, *lex* for Gaius is also "what the people orders and has established."

These facts, it seems to me, fully warrant Ihering's generalization when, for example, he says that the effect of a law for the citizen is that of a contract to which he has agreed, and the violation of a law is the breach of an obligation which he

49

has assumed. "The *lex publica* is a convention of all, and inversely a private convention is a law for the contracting parties." The law is a form of obligation binding the entire people; and, it might be added, binding each of them, because each is assumed to have assented to its enactment. Papinian, usually reckoned the greatest of Roman jurists, put this all in a single sentence: "*Lex* is a common engagement of the Republic (*communis rei publicae sponsio*)." [16] Now this *sponsio* was the essence of the old verbal contract at Rome, and Gaius tells us that its formal question, *Dari spondes?* and its answer, *Spondeo,* could be used by none but Roman citizens; while other formulae, such as *Dabis? Dabo,* might be used by other persons. Corresponding to these private *sponsiones* were the *rogationes* in which the whole people were asked if they were willing to assent to proposed legislation and thus make it binding law. And it was this consent alone that gave legal force to the measure proposed. Thus laws were spoken of as *leges rogatae.* A phrase of the *Lex Falcidia,* which we should naturally translate "after the enactment of this law," actually reads "post hanc legem *rogatam.*" [17] Enactment is thus termed "rogation," because the rogation contains the exact provision which the people turn into law when they accept it by their vote. But *rogatio,* like *sponsio,* had its private-law meaning too. *Rogo,* Gaius tells us, was one of the formal words by which a trust could be created in a will,[18] and other instances are numerous.

When Papinian speaks thus of a public law as a common engagement (*sponsio*) of the Republic, a common responsibility which the whole people have assumed, one cannot but believe that he must have been fully conscious of the political implications which the close parallel between the public and the private law inevitably brings to mind. Perhaps it should not be surprising that he met a violent death at the hands of the Emperor Caracalla.

But no account of Roman constitutionalism could be adequate which ignored the tendency toward autocracy in Roman institutions apparent even in the republican period. What impresses one here is the remarkable balancing of this tendency with the spirit of individual liberty which I have hitherto been trying to illustrate. Such a balancing is exemplified in the Roman distinction between the older *jus strictum* and the growing *jus honorarium,* and the remarkable fact that magisterial authority, the magistrates' *imperium,* becomes the chief medium of the liberalization of the law. Lawyers as a class are usually thought of as reactionary defenders of musty precedents, and sometimes they are. But I submit that there are few parallels in all intellectual history to the stupendous liberalization of Roman social institutions brought about by the generations of Roman jurists and magistrates, most of whom are unknown even by name; and this work was done largely by virtue of an authority, an *imperium,* which we must call in some sense arbitrary.

Thus a transfer of lands in strict law could be made only by a procedure so formal and intricate that the slightest slip would invalidate it, defeating the intentions of parties and what we should consider the ends of justice. No magistrate had authority to change this law, and till a comparatively late period it remained unchanged; but by authority of his *imperium* the magistrate could grant possession to the party "equitably" though not legally entitled to ownership, and could protect his possession until the law of prescription merged this possession in a full legal title. In this way the whole of property law was transformed and liberalized, and formality gave way to equitable considerations. It was nothing less than a gradual and silent social revolution, if we consider that a similar transformation was going on in every branch of law—the law of marriage, of family relations, of testamentary succession, of contracts, and, in fact, of all human relations.

There is probably no other social revolution in recorded history so important, so complete, so continuous over so long a period, as this evolution traceable step by step in the sources of Roman private law. We find institutions of an age long bygone still preserved in a law that is binding, but alongside it an actual administration enforcing principles often in many ways more advanced than those embodied in our own modern codes. Strict law tends to become a fiction, equity has become the important fact. The modern sociological school of jurists might, if they cared to look for it, find the strongest support for their theories in this remarkable evolution of Roman law. It is an interesting fact that Ihering, the greatest of early modern sociological jurists, left his *Geist des römischen Rechts* incomplete to pass on to the writing of his *Zweck im Recht*. The former naturally led him to the latter, and it is on the former rather than the latter that his reputation is likely to rest. It was the *imperium* no doubt that empowered the Roman magistrate to bring about such changes as these, but what we need to know is both how and why this *imperium* was used to strike off the shackles of the old formal law instead of strengthening them.

That subject is far too vast to be treated in a single lecture, but it suggests some parallels which may throw a little light on the general nature of Roman constitutional development. The parallel between Rome, on the one hand, and England and the British Empire on the other, has often been referred to; Ihering has noticed it, and Lord Bryce has developed it at some length in papers included in his two volumes of *Studies in History and Jurisprudence.* The parallel is very striking between the development of Rome under the Empire and that of Britain; particularly in the contrast noticeable in both between law and convention, and the resulting growth of what might be called "political fictions." But these parallels are usually drawn between two constitutional developments which appear very late in the national history both of Rome and of England. What we need in both cases is a study and a comparison of the earlier national characteristics which lie behind and may serve to explain their later striking similarities. That is a subject of much greater difficulty, and it has never yet been examined with the care it deserves and ought to receive. For I am convinced that the most fundamental likeness of Roman and British constitutionalism is a likeness resulting from a similarity of conditions which made English law a "common law," and made Roman law the law of the Italian peninsula. Before we compare Rome of the third or fourth century of the Christian era with Britain of the nineteenth, we ought to look for the similarities between republican Rome, and England in the period of corresponding growth during the three centuries following the Norman Conquest. It was the constitutional character of those relatively early periods of development in the two rival systems of common law which still dominates the western world; for in them were shaped those fundamental principles of both private and public law which constitute the true spirit of Roman and of English constitutionalism. The expansion of English law in southern Britain was a gradual process of incorporation of varied local customs in a system which in time thus became general and "common." The common law of England is an English *jus gentium* compounded of many pieces of local custom. In like fashion the *jus gentium* of Rome consisted of the legal principles "common" to the Italian states which Rome's expansion merged in the Roman judicial system. Among the unsung heroes of English constitutionalism are the great justiciars of Henry II, such as Richard de Lucy and Ranulf Glanvill, who were doing for English law what, centuries before, the long line of obscure but important *praetores peregrini* had done for the Roman.

The expansion of both the Roman and the English legal system called for great and fundamental changes at a time in the history of each when the law was still plastic but the process of law making was yet undeveloped. Thus the legal changes in twelfth- and thirteenth-century England and in the later centuries of the Roman Republic, far-reaching as both were, came to be the work of jurists rather than of legislators, and the mode of their expansion of the law came to be extension by way of juristic interpretation rather than addition through legislative action.

To a degree that seems unexampled for the time when it occurred, both Roman and English law thus became what we should term "judge-made" law, and to the end both systems exhibited the familiar characteristics of such law. One of the most marked of these characteristics was the great abundance of legal fictions which we find in both systems. Magistrates could not change the law, but they could stretch it to cover new circumstances by an untrue assumption of fact which no one was permitted to disprove. Such expedients tend to disappear, because less needed, when legal change becomes consciously legislative, as it finally did become in both Rome and England; and these archaic fictions have been the scorn of most modern legal reformers, notably Jeremy Bentham. But Bentham, like many of his fellows since his day, was much more noteworthy for his practical service in law reform than

54

for his historical sense. When an English court, in order to extend its jurisdiction beyond the limits of the ancient law, took notice of a bond executed "at Bordeaux in Islington in the County of Middlesex," or of the seizure of a vessel "on the high seas, to wit in Eastcheap in the City of London," this was a sign, not of the blindness of the courts, but of the backwardness of the legislature.

In still earlier periods, when legislative action was infrequent or even unthought of, these judicial fictions were the usual means by which judges tried to keep the law abreast of the times. The early history of law, both Roman and English, is full of them. Instances, though numerous in private law, are by no means confined to it. Where but in Rome during ancient times do we find a political fiction comparable to the Principate, "an absolute monarchy disguised by the forms of a commonwealth," as Gibbon calls it? Where but in England during modern times can we find an indigenous constitutional development in which the titular ruler is a king, the legal sovereign an assembly, and the ultimate political power a people? The Principate and the modern "limited monarchy" are alike fictions, and are the result of an age-long habit of thinking in fictions. The other great political fiction of the same class that comes to mind is the Holy Roman Empire; which, as Voltaire said, was not holy, not Roman, and not an empire. It was, however, much more Roman than holy, and its truly fictional character was purely Roman. And who but the Romans among the ancients would have "consulted the Senate" when the whole sovereignty lay in the *Comitia Centuriata?* Who but the English today would go on calling their court of final appeal the "House of Lords"? Or where except in England, or in a country with an English tradition, could one call the act of a king "unconstitutional" if he chose to exercise his undoubted legal discretion in withholding assent to a bill passed by both houses of parliament?

The constitutional or political habit at Rome which made possible the Principate seems to have been well-nigh unique in its time. There is much in the earlier history of Rome, institutional and intellectual, to prepare the way for it, but outside Rome apparently little or nothing. One cannot help wondering what Aristotle would have thought of the Roman Principate and under what form of government he would have classified it. Even in the most empirical and most practical parts of Aristotle's *Politics* there is nothing like the permanent antithesis of law and fact characteristic of the Roman Principate, or of the modern "limited" monarchy in which the king "reigns but does not rule." In Rome as in Greece there were revolutions, but in Rome a formal continuity was preserved, notwithstanding fundamental changes, that tended to disguise under older forms innovations which in Greece would have been open and avowed. It is interesting to see how much more frankly the new fact of the monarchy of the Caesars was recognized in the Greek provinces of Rome than in the West, and Ihering notes for an earlier period how often Greek writers on Roman history—such as Polybius, Dionysius of Halicarnassus, or Plutarch—consider as violations of law acts which to the Roman annalists are blamable but entirely within the law. The *mos majorum* forbade many things to a Roman for which there was no legal penalty. Convention, like fiction, played a large part in the development of Roman constitutionalism.

It is this general principle of continuity which helps to make clear the apparent paradox of the later Roman Empire, the retention by a despot like Justinian of writings alive with the spirit of constitutionalism. Few writings in the world's history have had the decisive influence of these lawbooks of Justinian. So much would probably be admitted on all hands, but with regard to the question whether on the whole this influence has been good or bad there is not the same unanimity, and to that question we must now turn.

From what has gone before it is evident that the first of my conclusions must be that the true essence of Roman constitutionalism does not lie in those late statements of absolutism to which so much currency has since been given, such as the maxim, *Quod principi placuit legis vigorem habet,* or Ulpian's assertion, *Princeps legibus solutus est.*[19] It lies in the older, deeper principle that the *populus,* and none but the whole *populus,* can be the ultimate source of legal authority. The fundamental doctrine underlying the Roman state, its true guiding spirit, is constitutionalism, not absolutism—a constitutionalism that Justinian's commissioners, even in the sixth century, could not delete from the legal sources, notwithstanding the Emperor's order to bring these sources up to date by addition, elimination, or change.

A second proposition may or may not prove to be more acceptable than this first: Before the Italian Renaissance, at least, the influence of Roman political institutions and ideas upon those of the developing states of western Europe was exercised through the legal compilations of Justinian more than through any other medium, even such a one as the history or general literature of Rome.

A third thesis will be recognized at once as more debatable, but I think it is defensible: The really decisive influence of Rome on later European politics came, not after the Italian Renaissance in the tendency toward absolutism, but during the middle ages in the reinforcement of constitutionalism.

If we confine ourselves strictly to matters legal and political, or at least to matters legal, the so-called Renaissance of the Twelfth Century appears more decisive in its ultimate influence than that later development to which we usually attach the word "Renaissance" *par excellence.*

In a brilliant lecture,[20] F. W. Maitland once pointed out the extent of the attack made upon the indigenous common law of England by the revived Roman law of the sixteenth century, and he might well have continued his study into the next century; but he recognized clearly that for England this Roman attack was an utter failure. English law was too "tough"; unlike the native law of Germany, it was already immune to foreign influence; it had been "inoculated" in the medieval period, and it was defended in the crisis by such staunch medievalists as Sir Edward Coke. Maitland attributes the persistence of the English common law very largely to the influence of the inns of court, and in this no doubt he is right; but the inns themselves were the result of an earlier development, and to me the really critical and decisive period in the competition of the native and the Roman law in England seems to come earlier, long before these societies of lawyers were founded, in the development of a common legal administrative system such as always results quickly in some kind of "common law." The common law that survived this belated attack of Romanism in the sixteenth century was of course a native English law, but it survived not because it was English but because it was "common"; or rather, because it had *become* "common," and that at a date relatively very early.

There was no mysterious quality in English custom, out of which our common law was made, to distinguish it from similar custom elsewhere; it had no "manifest destiny" to become as it did the unique rival of Rome in the legal systems of the later western world. Its ultimate victory over Romanism was not

58

the result of any inherent superiority, Wycliffe and Sir John Fortescue to the contrary notwithstanding. That victory was won by the end of the thirteenth century, and the issue was really determined in the twelfth. If Irnerius had taught, or Azo had written, a century before he did, or if a Henry III instead of a Henry II had followed Stephen on the throne of England, we might well be using the *Digest* of Justinian as a text today in our American law schools. It was not the merits of English custom, but the uniform writs and the itinerant justices of Henry II, that made this custom the "law of the land." And if those English justices of the twelfth century had been as fully versed in the law of Rome as the German judges were in the fifteenth, an English "reception" of Roman law in the thirteenth century seems no more startling or unlikely as a consequence than the later German one.

Law, however, is one thing, jurisprudence quite another. Law is the material of jurisprudence, jurisprudence the rationalization of law. The law may come from one source, the jurisprudence from another. In the early sixteenth century the English jurist Christopher Saint-German divided the law of England, or more properly her jurisprudence, into "the law of reason primary and the law of reason secondary." [21]

In this division he was no doubt influenced by St. Thomas' distinction between the ultimate principles of the universal and unchangeable law of nature, on the one hand, and, on the other, the specific deductions that men may make from these general principles. Such secondary deductions concerning the law of property—and the law of property then included probably four-fifths of all law—when actually found among all nations, Saint-German calls "the law of reason secondary general, for the law of property is generally kept in all countries"; whereas

The law of reason secondary particular is the law that is derived of divers customs general and particular, and of divers maxims and statutes ordained in this realm. And it is called the law of reason secondary particular, because the reason in that case is derived of such a law that is only holden for law in this realm, and in none other realm.

This is little more than an extension of the statement of Gaius: "All peoples who are ruled by laws and customs employ a law partly peculiar to themselves, partly common to all mankind." [22] Saint-German's "law of reason secondary general" is in fact the *jus gentium* of Gaius.

In the earlier formative period of the English common law we do undoubtedly find not only pure English custom but a rationalization of it, a jurisprudence which might be called native, an English "law of reason secondary particular." But as Saint-German clearly implies, these "particular" deductions are and must be only a limited application of the universally accepted principles of the "law of reason secondary general." To put it in more familiar language, a given country may have its own particular laws and even its particular jurisprudence, but this jurisprudence cannot but be consonant with a jurisprudence that is general and universal.

Yet whatever a nation's peculiar laws may be, few, I think, could doubt the truth of the statement of Édouard Cuq, quoted above, that "the Romans have fixed for all time the categories of juristic thought." The "law of reason secondary general" of England, as of every other western European country, was a law, or rather a rationalization of law, permeated by the juridical conceptions of Rome.

In the formation of our common law these Roman conceptions have therefore, as it seems to me, a place no less significant than the English custom they served to rationalize. They came to England too late, no doubt, to replace the English customary law itself, but they did come in time to have a large part in the orderly arrangement and development of that law and in the "law of reason secondary particular" derived from it.

The failure always to distinguish thus between matter and form may be the explanation of the wide difference in the estimates modern legal historians give of the extent of the Roman element in English law. Sir Henry Maine asserted that Bracton had palmed off as English a law of which a full third was Roman; but according to Maitland "a thirtieth" would have been nearer the mark.[23] Any attempt to give a quantitative ratio of two things as different as the matter and the form of law is likely to be inconclusive.

In this long discussion of law it might seem that we had lost sight of the constitution. But in the middle ages the connection between private and public law was far closer than it is now; and in early English, as in early Roman institutions, we must look for much of the spirit of the constitution in the developing principles of what we now think of as only a single branch of private law, the law of property. For the medieval law of property was also the law of franchises or "liberties," of personal status, of public office, and of much more besides. For example, even so constitutional a thing as the king's prerogative, when it became the subject of judicial discussion, was treated in the courts under the same general rules as the proprietary right of any subject, and this almost to the very eve of what we call the modern period. In France of the thirteenth century, according to Beaumanoir, the king has the sovereignty over his kingdom, but so, he says, has every individual baron over his barony.[24]

In conclusion therefore I shall add two more heretical generalizations to the ones I have hitherto been trying to defend and illustrate. The first is that, to reach a true conception of the spirit of our constitutional antecedents in the middle ages, the jurisprudence is at least equal in importance to the mere subject matter of the law. I do not question here the English character or the early origin of the bulk of our common law; above all, I would not minimize the decisive influence of the ancient English County Court; I only say that the constitutional implications may come as much—if not indeed even more—from the law's later rationalization as from its original character. The second proposition is that this jurisprudence, as distinct from that law, is pretty largely Roman in its derivation, though considered in the middle ages probably not so much specifically Roman as "common to all mankind." The third and last is that the central political principle of this Roman jurisprudence is not, as has so often been assumed, the absolutism of a prince, but the doctrine that the people is the ultimate source of all legitimate political authority in a state.

The last of these propositions perhaps requires the most proof, for it has been most frequently disputed. "Few texts," says the late Professor Esmein, "have exercised an influence more profound upon the development of the public law in certain countries of Europe, and above all in France," than the Roman maxim, *princeps legibus solutus est;* [25] but he admits that England "has had the good fortune to escape that influence." [26] This unusual good fortune, when admitted, is usually attributed to the free institutions of Anglo-Saxon England, to an unexplained development of the representative parliament in the later middle ages, or to some mysterious quality in the English blood or character that makes for liberty. The threat of absolutism, when it came—as of course it did—came from the despotic doctrines of the Roman law, which was "reborn" with everything else at the close of the middle ages. This is the theory that is generally current.

For the period immediately after the Conquest in England the evidence on which one must rest the conclusions just stated, or the different conclusions which I prefer, is slight, scattered, and rather inconclusive—a few stray sentences occurring incidentally here and there in the legal writings of the period, of which the so-called *Leges Henrici Primi* is easily the most important. Just at the end of the Norman period, in the only book of pure Roman law written in medieval England, in the Prologue of the *Liber Pauperum* of Vacarius, we find a repetition of some of the statements of the first title of Justinian's *Digest* concerning the source of law, including the one that the emperor is its only establisher and interpreter. But the book of Vacarius was written entirely in the spirit of the early glossators; it is purely antiquarian and Roman and makes practically no reference to English law or its relation to the law of Rome.[27]

For concrete evidence of much value we have to wait till the reign of Henry II in the *De Legibus et Consuetudinibus Angliae* attributed to Ranulf Glanvill, Henry's chief justiciar during his later years, and written after the enactment of the king's great administrative reforms. Glanvill's prologue contains certain statements of the greatest interest. It is evident that the author considers this book as a kind of English equivalent of Justinian's *Institutes,* and his prologue is clearly modeled on that of Justinian though the book itself is not. A comparison of the two prologues is instructive both for their similarities and their differences. After a mention of the need for laws as well as for arms, each has a paragraph recounting the military achievements of the ruler, and then proceeds to a

summary statement concerning the laws. The last of these
alone is important here. Justinian's summary refers only to the
written law and the compilations of it made at his order. The
one in Glanvill must in part be given in its own words. In the
king's court each decision, it says, is governed by the laws of
the realm (*legibus regni*) [28] and by customs (*consuetudinibus*) drawn from reason and long observed; and in these decisions the king does not disdain to consult those of his subjects
whom he knows to stand out by their virtue, "by their skill
in the law, and by the customs of the realm" (*morum gravitate,
in peritia juris et regni consuetudinibus*). On this follows the
sentence most significant of all:

For it should not be thought absurd to call the English laws *leges*
although not written—why, *quod principi placet legis habet vigorem*, even that is a *lex!*—those, I mean, which have manifestly
been promulgated concerning doubtful points determinable in the
council, with the advice at least of the magnates and under authority of the prince.[29]

The reasoning of the author is here so closely parallel to
that of a remarkable sentence or two in the *Digest* that I think
he must have read them. They occur in an extract from the
great Roman jurist of the second century, Salvius Julianus,
compiler of the famous *Edictum Perpetuum*, and in the following words:

Immemorial custom is observed as *lex*, and not without reason; and
this is the law which is said to be established by usage. For since
leges themselves are binding on us for no other reason than that
they have been received by the judgment of the people, it is proper
that those things of which the people have approved without any
writing shall also be binding on everyone. After all, what is the
difference whether the people makes known its will by a vote, or
by the things themselves and by acts? [30]

One other interesting bit of evidence of Glanvill's attitude toward absolutism may be worth citing. The chronicler of the abbey of Abingdon tells us that in 1185, on the death of the abbot, Henry II entrusted the abbey to one Thomas of Esseburn, who thereupon proposed to hand over to the king the whole of the possessions of the abbey, including those of the prior and convent. The prior and brothers appealed to Glanvill, the chief justiciar, insisting that the possessions of the prior and convent should be excepted; and, says the chronicler,

The grace of God finally prevailed to this extent, that Rannulphus de Glanvilla, the chief of the justices, turning to the other justices, said that our customary rights had been established reasonably and wisely, that nothing excessive could be found in them, *and that the lord king neither wishes* NOR DARES to go against customs in some measure so ancient and so just or to change anything respecting them.

All the justices "who were seated around" agreed after a conference, and the *curia* decided unanimously in favor of the prior and brothers. The king "neither wishes *nor dares!*" And all the justices concurred! [31]

Whether Glanvill wrote the treatise attributed to him will perhaps never be known, but his own constitutional views were probably representative, and they were certainly not despotic. Nevertheless, the reference in Glanvill's prologue to the maxim *quod principi placuit legis habet vigorem*, as quoted above, has been cited as proof of the absolutist doctrines both of Glanvill and of England in his time. To infer from that incidental and left-handed reference to the Roman maxim the author's out-and-out endorsement of it seems to me only another striking proof of the fertility of the human imagination. Yet that inference has been made. I might almost say it has prevailed. It seems to me obvious, on the other hand, for reasons particularly set forth above, that this twelfth-century English jurist has seen more clearly than some modern historians the true central principle of the Roman constitution— which was not absolutism, but the doctrine that the *populus* is the sole source of law; that he believes this principle to apply no less to English institutions than to Roman; and, finally, that these constitutional doctrines of his are fairly representative of the ones held and enforced in medieval England.

Further reasons for the conclusions above are to be found in the explicit statements of Bracton some sixty years after Glanvill; but with Bracton the immediate subject of the present lecture becomes merged in the wider topic of English constitutionalism generally, and may be treated more clearly later as a part of that topic.

CHAPTER IV

Constitutionalism
in the Middle Ages

BETWEEN Glanvill at the end of the twelfth century and
Bracton in the middle of the next the development of English
governmental institutions goes on apace, and some incidental
light on their spirit could no doubt be got from a careful study
of the contemporary records of the law cases which now become available. But of the true character of the general principles underlying the medieval English constitution there is
no indication so clear as the book on the laws and customs of
England by Henry of Bratton, or Bracton—the greatest of
medieval books on English law and constitutionalism, if not
on the law of any European nation.

Bracton's book is a book of case law; it is probably, as has
been said, the unique medieval book of case law, and without
doubt that case law is almost entirely an English law. But no
attentive reader of the book can miss in it the great influence
of a jurisprudence that is far older and far wider than any
mere "law of reason secondary," and "particular" to England.
All this has been so admirably stated by the greatest master
of our medieval legal history that I take the liberty of quoting
a brilliant passage in place of a bad summary:

"If for one moment we set his [Bracton's] book beside the
Customs of Beauvais and the Saxon Mirror," says Maitland,
one fact worthy of note stares us in the face. The Englishman's
work both in its general structure and in many details has been

influenced by Roman jurisprudence. Really if we place ourselves in the thirteenth century and look only at the surface of things, it must seem very likely that England will soon adopt Roman law as a whole, while into Northern France and Germany it will make its way but slowly or never. After the event we can see why such a prediction would be foolish. The development in England of a centralized royal justice was rapid, precocious. Before the end of the thirteenth century the system with its stubborn writs and formulas had become too osseous to be much modified by new outlandish learning. And looking closer we see that Bracton had no intention of supplanting English by Roman law. It is Rationalism rather than Romanism that he learnt from Azo's book, and this fact that at an early date English law was rationalized by an able man, is not the least among the causes which protected us against Romanism in the following centuries.

Trying to state in general terms . . . what was Bracton's debt to the civilians we may put it thus:—First he had learned certain wide principles of jurisprudence, had found some of the highest premisses of all civilized law expressed in neat and accurate phrases. For these, at least for some of these, the England of his time was ripe. They are not, he might argue, specifically Roman; the Romans themselves regarded them as common to all mankind; they are dictates of reason implicit in all law. . . . Then there are instances in which rules that are less general and more specifically Roman are adopted, or rather proposed, as solutions for concrete cases. . . . But the main debt is less palpable, for what he has converted to his use is spirit rather than substance, not these or those rules, but a method of reasoning about law, of perceiving the interdependence of rules, of making them take their places as members of a body.[1]

The "spirit" that animated Bracton's book includes the public as well as the private law, and I find it hard to distinguish this spirit from the *Geist des römischen Rechts.*

Among the extracts from Bracton's book that most directly concern our present subject, we may dismiss the famous statement, so often repeated in the English constitutional struggle of the seventeenth century, that the king has a superior, not only in God and in the law which makes him king, but in his *curia* as well—in the earls and barons who are his associates there—"and one who has an associate has a master; and therefore if the King is without a bridle, that is without law, they ought to put a bridle on him." Modern research in the manuscripts of Bracton has shown that this rather startling doctrine is no statement of Bracton's, but an addition by another hand, made probably by some adherent of the baronial party opposed to Henry III.[2]

There are, however, enough genuine statements of Bracton from which his essential constitutional views may be perceived. From what has been said earlier of Roman constitutionalism it will be evident that one of the most significant of these statements is Bracton's quotation, word for word, of the dictum of Papinian, "*Lex* is a common engagement of the republic (*communis rei publicae sponsio*)," [3] and his application of it to English law. About the same time a jurist of Orléans was quoting the same passage in a French form.[4] Another example occurs in Bracton's *Introductio*, which is in part a paraphrase of Glanvill's Prologue:

Moreover, while in almost all regions they use *leges* and a written law, England alone employs within her boundaries an unwritten law and custom. In this at least without a writing what usage has approved becomes law. But it will not be absurd to call the English laws *leges* even when unwritten, since whatever is justly defined and approved with the counsel and consent of the magnates and the common engagement (*sponsio*) of the republic, the authority of the King or prince preceding, should have the force of a *lex*. . . . The English *leges* and customs, by the authority of kings, sometimes command, sometimes forbid, sometimes take vengeance and inflict a penalty upon transgressors. These laws, since they have been approved by the consent of those using them and confirmed by the oath of kings, can neither be changed nor destroyed without the common consent of all those with whose counsel and consent they have been promulgated.[5]

In dealing with the Roman constitution we have already noticed the maxim of Ulpian, "What has pleased the prince has the force of a *lex*." [6] It has the force of law because the *populus* confers on the prince its whole *imperium* and *potestas* (*cum lege regia . . . populus ei et in eum omne suum imperium et potestatem conferat*). Bracton's treatment of this important passage is so remarkable that we must examine it in some detail. This is his statement:

For the king has no other power in his lands, since he is the minister and vicar of God, save that alone which he has of right (*de jure*). Nor is that to the contrary where it is said *quod principi placet legis habet vigorem*, for there follows at the end of the law *cum lege regia quae de imperio eius lata est* (together with the *lex regia* which has been laid down concerning his authority). Therefore it is not anything rashly presumed by will of the king, but what has been rightly defined with the king's authorization on the advice of his magnates after deliberation and conference concerning it.[7]

It is worth comparing Justinian's statement of the principle with this later gloss of Bracton. Where the former says the prince's will has the force of a *lex* "because" (*cum*) the people by a *lex regia* have conceded to him the whole of their authority, Bracton says it has the force of a law "in accordance with a *lex regia* (*cum lege regia*) which had been made." In the

70

Institutes the *cum* is a particle introducing a clause which gives merely an historical reason for a complete and arbitrary authority actually in the emperor; whereas in our Bractonian text the *cum* is a preposition governing a noun in the ablative. Justinian says the prince's will is law, because (*cum*) the people have conceded all their power to him; the existing text of Bracton says the prince's will is law together with, or if in accordance with the *lex regia* (*cum lege regia*); and this *lex regia* admits of nothing beyond a true definition of what the law already is, promulgated by the king's authority only after discussion with the magnates and on their advice. Justinian's is a doctrine of practical absolutism; Bracton's seems to be a clear assertion of constitutionalism. In the one the prince's will actually is law, in the other it is only an authoritative promulgation by the king of what the magnates declare to be the ancient custom. No doubt Bracton was acquainted with the true wording of the original text, and his own book is conclusive proof of his skill in the Latin tongue; and yet our text of Bracton, in quoting this plain statement of absolutism, turns it into an assertion of constitutionalism by such heroic means as changing a causal conjunctive into a preposition and omitting entirely the reference in the original to the concession of the people's whole power to the prince.

So far as I recall, attention has never been drawn to the significant fact that this passage in Bracton follows immediately upon a quotation of the English coronation oath and serves as a commentary on it. The inference seems obvious that Bracton considered the oath taken by the kings of England at their coronation in some ways analogous to the *lex regia* by which the Roman emperors at their accession had received the *imperium* and *potestas* of the people; the king's coronation oath is in fact Bracton's English *lex regia*. But it is no *lex regia* which, like that of the *Institutes,* confers on the prince the people's entire authority. On the contrary, it limits any authority the prince may have to acts in conformity with its solemn promises, and within little more than half a century after the appearance of Bracton's book, if not earlier, these promises included an engagement to govern according to the laws which the people have chosen (*quas vulgus elegerit*).[8] Thus, says our text of Bracton, it is only when an expression of the prince's will is in conformity with this *lex regia* that his will becomes a binding law; and this the oath restricts to the official judgments or decrees of the kings' *curia.* Later, French liberal jurists were to employ somewhat the same argument when they interpreted the royal words, *car tel est nôtre plaisir,* to mean merely *placitum est.*[9]

It seems clear from this evidence that for Bracton the English monarchy was far from a despotism such as Justinian's. There are, however, other words of his which have been thought to point to a very different conclusion. In the same passage from which I have just been quoting Bracton says that the king "ought not to have a peer, much less a superior," and then goes on to quote from Justinian's *Code* the famous *Digna vox* of the Emperors Theodosius and Valentinian: "It is a worthy voice of reigning majesty to profess that the prince is bound by the laws"—which seems properly to indicate nothing more than a check upon the prince's actions imposed by himself alone and of his own free will. In another passage, which seems undoubtedly genuine, Bracton says that "neither justices nor private persons ought or can dispute concerning royal charters and royal acts." "No one can pass judgment on a charter or an act of the king, so as to make void the king's act." [10] The king is under no man (*non sub homine*), even if he is under God and the law.[11]

72

The apparent contradiction disclosed here between these different statements of Bracton led in later centuries to a two-fold tradition, one constitutional, the other absolutist. In the great state trials under the Stuarts involving alleged infringement by the king of the subjects' rights or liberties, Bracton is almost invariably quoted by both opponents and defenders of the royal prerogative, and all these quotations seem plausible. In 1627, for instance, in Darnel's Case, which resulted in the Petition of Right, on the question of release on bail of a subject imprisoned on an order of the king showing no cause of arrest, Calthrop, counsel for one of the prisoners, quoted Bracton's statement that the king can do nothing save what is done according to law; while Heath, Attorney General, ended a long speech for the king by saying:

I shall conclude what I shall say on this case . . . with the words of Bracton, who spake not to flatter the present age, . . . *Si judicium a rege testatur (cum breve non currat contra ipsum) locus erat supplicationi quod factum suam corrigat et emendet.* . . . My lord, I English it not, for I apply it not; any man may make use of it as he pleaseth.

Possibly I had better "English it." "If a judgment is attested by the king [i.e., a decision infringing the legal right of a subject] (since no writ runs against the king) there was opportunity of supplication that he might correct and amend his act." [12]

It is somewhat surprising that historians have been content to leave such an apparent discrepancy as this so largely unexplained. Was Bracton, then, an absolutist or a constitutionalist, or was he just a blockhead? This is our question. If we were to frame that question in terms of the institutions and ideas of the twentieth century, or possibly even of the seventeenth, "blockhead" might seem the only reasonable answer. It seems impossible that the same man, if a sane man, could declare that the king has no peer on earth, much less a superior, and that no subject, not even a judge, can question or ought to question the legality of any of his acts; and could then go on to add that the king's will is not law except in the form of a definition to which the assent of the magnates is absolutely essential. For if the latter were true, must it not follow, as the annotator of one of Bracton's manuscripts said, that a prince who must act in concert with such companions in reality has a master who may "put a bridle on him"? Is not the medieval English monarchy then a mixed and not a pure monarchy? This is the principal riddle, not of Bracton alone, but of medieval constitutionalism generally, and a solution of it is the first essential for an understanding of this important stage in our constitutional history, and, I think I may add without exaggeration, of almost every stage subsequent to this.

The riddle of Bracton is in reality the riddle of our medieval constitutionalism. If I can offer any solution at all, it will be more concrete and more convincing, I think, if I first try it on the text of Bracton and then if possible give illustrations of its wider aspects. Now there is one great passage in Bracton which, to my mind, gives the key to his own reconciliation of the two apparently contradictory views we have been noticing, and I cannot find that historians have given all parts of it the attention they deserve, although they have often discussed some parts and other passages at great length. For, as it seems to me, this passage contains nothing less than the solution of the great problem of our medieval constitutionalism, and it will be necessary to read it. I would spare you these dry details if I could, but I know of no safe road by which we may arrive at true generalizations in history except the narrow and sometimes devious path through the concrete details, and by the most minute and careful examination of them. Generalizations without such a basis—and we have too many of them—are not merely worthless; they are often in their practical results very dangerous.

The passage to which I have referred occurs in a book dealing with the acquisition of dominion over external goods, and Bracton first treats of corporeal goods and then turns to incorporeal, such as "rights" and "liberties." In his treatment of the latter, in the twenty-fourth chapter of his second book,[13] the author considers the question as to who may grant liberties and which ones belong to the king. "Now," he says,

in the matter of liberties, we must consider who is able to grant them, to whom and in what manner they are transferred, in what way they are in possession or quasi possession, and how they are retained by user. Who, then? And you must know that it is the lord king himself, who has the ordinary jurisdiction and dignity and power over all who are in his realm. For he has in his hand all rights touching the crown, and the secular power, and the material sword which pertains to the governance of the realm (*qui pertinet ad regni gubernaculum*). Moreover he has the justice and the judgment belonging to his jurisdiction, so that by virtue of his jurisdiction as minister and vicar of God he attributes (*tribuat*) to each one what is his own. He has also those things which concern the peace, in order that the people entrusted to him may live in quiet and repose, that none should beat or wound or maltreat another, that none should take or carry away another's goods, that no one should maim or kill a man. For he has coercive power to punish and compel wrongdoers. Likewise he has it in his power in his own person to observe and to make his subjects observe the enactments and decrees and assizes provided, approved, and sworn to in his realm (*leges et constitutiones et assisas in regno suo provisas et approbatas et iuratas*).

75

Note particularly that last phrase indicating the kinds of enactment which the king is free to observe or ignore at his pleasure—and note not merely what Bracton includes but also what he omits. It is not by accident, I think, that an enactment defining *consuetudo* or custom does not accompany *constitutio* in this list. "For," as the author continues,

it is useless to establish rights if there is no one to maintain rights. Therefore the king has the rights of this kind, or jurisdictions, in his hand. In addition he has in preference to all others in his realm privileges of his own under the *jus gentium* which are owing by the law of nature, such as treasure trove, etc.

Then, after enumerating such privileges, he goes on:

Those things which belong to jurisdiction and the peace, and those which are incidental to justice or the peace, pertain to no one except to the crown alone and to the royal dignity; nor can they be separated from the crown, since they constitute the crown itself. For the *esse* of the crown is to exercise justice and judgment and to maintain the peace; and without these the crown could neither subsist nor endure. Moreover the rights of this kind, or jurisdictions, cannot be transferred to persons or to fiefs; they cannot be in the possession of a private person, neither the enjoyment nor the exercise of the right, except where this has been granted to him from above as a delegated jurisdiction, and it cannot be delegated in such a way as to prevent the ordinary jurisdiction's remaining in the king himself. On the other hand those things known as privileges (*privilegia*), though they pertain to the crown, may be separated from it and transferred to private persons, but only by special grace of the king himself. If his grace and special concession should not appear, lapse of time does not exclude the king from such a claim. For time does not run against him in this case where there is no need of proof. For it ought to be clear to all that things of this kind pertain to the crown unless there is someone who can prove the contrary by producing a special grant. In other matters, where proof is necessary, time runs against the king just as it would against any others.

I think it is fair to say that in these few remarkable sentences we find the whole sum of the English polity, and of even more than the merely English polity, in the middle of the thirteenth century. But if these statements are now combined with the others already quoted, the following propositions among others may, I think, be legitimately deduced as a solution of the Bractonian dilemma, and even as a tentative outline of our medieval constitutionalism.

In Bracton's discussion of these questions the order may not be logically the best, but it seems advisable generally to follow it. First, he says, the king has in his hand the government (*gubernaculum*) of the realm. The significant fact is that acts of government strictly defined are in the hands of the king alone. There he "has no peer, much less a superior." No one, not even a judge, can question a specifically royal act so as to bring its legitimacy into doubt. There is here a separation far sharper than we make in our modern times between government and law, between *gubernaculum* and *jurisdictio*. And in government thus more narrowly defined the king not only is the sole administrator, but he has of right and must have all powers needed for an effective administration; he has "in his hand" all things incidental or "annexed" to government. I am reminded of a striking statement of Bracton's great Italian contemporary Egidio Colonna, who says that the king should have "a fullness of civil power (*abundare in civili potentia*) in order to be able to control those who would rise in revolt and disturb the peace of the realm." [14] Bracton's English constitutional principle is in fact nothing but a commonplace of late thir-

77

teenth-century European political theory. And of all Bracton's constitutional statements this is probably the most fundamental. Government does not include jurisdiction in our narrower definition of the latter word. In this government and the things annexed thereto the king is properly an autocrat; he is "absolute"; he has no peer; his strictly governmental acts are beyond question. Within that sphere no act of his can be illegal, because within it his discretionary power is legitimate, complete, and shared by none. All government is the king's government and there is no other.

Possibly one reason for Bracton's reiteration of this fundamental doctrine was the fact that it was questioned at the very time when he was finishing the writing of his book, about 1259. The Provisions of Oxford of 1258 were a striking practical application of the contrary theory, that the earls and barons, fellow members with the king in his *curia*, were his equals and collectively even his superiors—not in jurisdiction alone, which was admitted, but in government as well—and that if necessary they might "put a bridle on him," as the later "addition" to Bracton's text puts it. Such was certainly not the view of Bracton, and apparently it was not the view generally accepted throughout England or Europe in the thirteenth century. Though it was repeated in the English lawbook known as *Fleta* in the reign of Edward I, Edward's adherents had repudiated it in the *Dictum de Kenilworth* before his father's death, and his own later policy as king shows no traces of it. The decision of St. Louis in 1264 against the Provisions of Oxford was dictated by a political doctrine which is in all important respects the same as Bracton's.

One of the essential features of Bracton's constitutionalism undoubtedly is the clear-cut separation he thus makes between *gubernaculum* and *jurisdictio*, allowing the king an autocratic and irresponsible authority within the former, but never beyond it. It is also the one important feature of our medieval constitution which above all others modern political developments have tended most to obscure. The debates in parliament and in Westminster Hall even in the early seventeenth century show plainly that the men of the time, whether unconsciously or intentionally, frequently blur this distinction which so colors the whole of Bracton's constitutional views. They cite without discrimination his statements as conclusive proof, either of an almost complete royal absolutism, or of a direct parliamentary control in Bracton's age; to neither of which Bracton himself could possibly have subscribed, even if he had understood it.

No doubt partisanship accounts in part for these one-sided interpretations, but it by no means accounts for all; and it accounts still less for the fact that subsequent historians, even some recent ones, have taken almost as little account of this prime principle of medieval constitutionalism as the heated controversialists of the time of the Stuarts. The changing world always makes earlier times incomprehensible. In the apt words of Sir Henry Spelman,

When states are departed from their original Constitution, and that original by tract of time worn out of Memory; the succeeding Ages viewing what is past by the present, conceive the former to have been like to that they live in; and framing thereupon erroneous Propositions, do likewise make thereon erroneous Inferences and Conclusions.[15]

In this particular case some of Bracton's own illustrations of "governmental" action may have contributed to the later misunderstanding, especially his apparent inclusion of royal charters among those things annexed to "government" and therefore "not fit for the tongue of any lawyer"; or his assertion above, which seems to imply that it lies within the king's discretion (*habet in potestate sua*) whether to obey or to enforce obedience to such important forms of legal enactment as *leges, constitutiones,* and *assisae.* It must be confessed that medieval English history as a whole does seem to show that a royal charter promising reform in "government" was seldom better than a "scrap of paper"; nor is there anything in Bracton's theory itself to make it legally enforceable.

A striking proof of the accuracy of Bracton's statements concerning these charters of "government" occurred in 1223. In a *colloquium* or parliament of that year, Archbishop Langton urges young Henry III to observe the promises of reform in government made in the earlier reissue of Magna Carta; but even he does not say the king is legally bound to do so. He only says that the king, and all the nobility with him, have taken a solemn oath to observe *"omnes libertates praescriptas."* [16] At most, in matters of public administration rather than private right, if the two could be distinguished in a feudal period, he seems to imply no more than a moral obligation on the king's part to observe a promise under oath. This is no legal restriction on the king's power. If he issues a charter promising reforms in the royal government, he is bound only by the moral obligation of the *Digna vox* to stand by his oath. That view was stated in its baldest form by William Brewer, one of the oldest and most experienced of the members of the *curia,* who answered Langton on behalf of the young king thus: "The liberties which you have demanded ought not to be observed as a matter of right (*de jure*), because they have been extorted by violence." In his reply to this Langton does not assert any obligation *de jure.* He only upbraids Brewer for endangering the peace of the realm. In conclusion the king gave way to

Langton, but he conceded nothing whatever as a matter of right: "All those liberties we have sworn to and for all we are bound, so that we will observe what we have taken oath to." It is noteworthy that in the reissue of the Charter which Henry finally made in 1225 in response to these repeated complaints, he says explicitly that he is conceding the liberties demanded only of his own free will (*spontanea et bona voluntate nostra*).[17] He concedes absolutely nothing as a matter of right. Whether justifiable or not, this interpretation of the "constitution" is the one held by St. Louis,[18] and by the framers of the *Dictum de Kenilworth* [19] containing the terms of pacification after the fall of Simon de Montfort.

Bracton's assertion concerning royal charters seems on the whole to have had the support of precedent. But in a feudal period, such as this was, "private" rights and public law are so interwoven that the line is hard to draw between such *libertates praescriptae* as belong to the king alone as a part of the "government" over which he has *plenam potestatem et liberum regimen*—in the phrase of St. Louis [20]—and, on the other hand, those prescriptive rights of tenants or subjects which are wholly outside and beyond the legitimate bounds of royal administration and fall properly under *jurisdictio,* not under *gubernaculum.* As to the latter rights, those which we in modern times should be tempted to call "private" or "individual," the principles of the law are perfectly clear; and charters concerning these alone are vastly different from those, such as some parts of Magna Carta, which had been wrung from an unwilling king by force and involved a real diminution of royal or strictly "governmental" authority. True, as Bracton says, interpretation of even a "private" charter, when ambiguous or uncertain, is forbidden to the judges; that right belongs only to the king who made it, if he is alive. But the legal aspect

81

of such a charter is clearly within the sphere of *jurisdictio,* not of *gubernaculum,* and Bracton says plainly that the judges will quash the charter if it infringes rights contained in an earlier grant, whether made by the same king or by a predecessor, provided there has been no loss of the earlier right by nonuser. So much seems clear in principle. Nor is the principle without practical consequences. Although no writ runs against the king himself, title to a hereditament, corporeal or incorporeal, if derived from an extralegal grant of the king, is bad, and in many cases the king's justices so decided. Obviously, the king can do wrong, even if the penalty can, in Bracton's phrase, be exacted by none but God the avenger.

A greater suspicion of Bracton's constitutionalism might, however, naturally arise from his statement above about the decrees and assizes which he also appears to annex to "government." If, as Bracton seems to imply, it is within the king's legitimate discretion to disregard these important enactments of law, "approved and sworn to" in his realm, how possibly can the English king be other than a prince *solutus legibus?*

Again, like St. Thomas Aquinas, I would solve the problem by making a distinction—and this is another of those medieval constitutional distinctions almost as important as that between government and jurisdiction, and unfortunately almost as often overlooked in modern times—namely, the distinction between an enactment of administrative procedure, on the one hand, and, on the other, a definition of legal right. This distinction is fundamental with Bracton, but has been forgotten by us. To him *leges* (in the narrow sense of the word), *constitutiones,* and *assisae* are nothing more than administrative orders and therefore a part of "government"—something which "pertains to the administration of the realm (*pertinet ad regni gubernaculum*)" [21]—and as such are properly within

82

the king's exclusive control. Definitions of "right," on the other hand, share the character of the immemorial custom they define, and these, Bracton says, "since they have been approved by the consent of those using them and confirmed by the oath of kings, can neither be changed nor destroyed without the common consent of all those with whose counsel and consent they have been promulgated." [22] This is another apparent contradiction in Bracton, but like the former one we noticed, I hope to be able to show that it is a contradiction of our own making.

Proofs of the accuracy of this distinction made by Bracton, and of its great importance in medieval England and elsewhere, are scattered all through the historical sources of the period, official and nonofficial. The earliest clear case I recall is one in the *Curia Regis* during Stephen's reign, in which the justices quashed a royal order of Henry I which infringed certain rights of Battle Abbey granted by the Conqueror. [23] A king might be strong enough to enforce such an illegal provision during his own life, as the *Dialogue of the Exchequer* suggests, [24] but it is none the less illegal. The closing words of Henry II's great assize of Clarendon of 1166, "and the lord King wills that this assize shall be binding in his realm *as long as pleases him*," [25] show that this was one of those enactments which the king, as Bracton says, has in his own discretion (*habet in potestate sua*). [26] But its content is administrative only, and from a very early time it was clearly recognized that a right, or a custom defining such a right, or an official promulgation of what such a custom truly means, was a far different thing from these mere administrative orders. Such a custom, Glanvill said, the king does not will and does not *dare* to change. [27] When all courts of law had been finally absorbed in the royal jurisdiction as they had been by Bracton's time, no writ ran against the king; and a right, if against the king, could be made good only by petition. Nevertheless, an infringement by the king was a wrong and the law clearly recognized it as such.[28] When recorded cases become available, they furnish innumerable instances of the principle from the opening of the thirteenth century to the end of the middle ages and afterward.

Of all the discretionary powers of the crown, the maintenance of the peace was practically the most important on account of the general disorder of the time. To maintain peace was one of the three things to which the king was bound in the coronation oath. Peace and justice are the two things that make the crown what it is, says Bracton; they above everything else constitute the *raison d'être* of kingship. Peace and those powers necessary to its maintenance are, therefore, wholly within the king's control. Many other aspects of "government" prominent in modern times, such as foreign relations, do not come within Bracton's purview, but the general principles of his politics may be gathered from his treatment of the few which were most important in his day.

From these things which the king has within his discretion, his *gubernaculum*, we must now turn to the ones that fall under Bracton's correlative term, *jurisdictio*. The word *jurisdictio*, like *lex*, is used by Bracton sometimes with a wide, sometimes with a narrower meaning. In its widest sense it embraces no less than the whole of the king's authority, but in many places it is clearly used in distinction to *gubernatio* or *gubernaculum*, the two together constituting the whole of the powers of the crown. Like government proper, jurisdiction is in constitutional theory a monopoly of the crown and inseparable from it. All jurisdiction is a delegation from the king. It may be said that by Bracton's time the king is "the fountain of justice," and in no respect was the institution of kingship more fully warranted than in the administration of justice. There were, of course, many courts which were not the king's courts, but the rights of subjects were ultimately protected by royal writs, through which cases might be transferred to the royal courts on the ground of a failure or a defect of justice. And in view of the effectiveness of these royal remedies, Bracton's assertion that all jurisdiction was the king's jurisdiction, exercised directly or through delegation—fiction though it was— came nearer to being an actual fact in England at that time than it did in some other parts of Western Europe for centuries.

The aspect of *jurisdictio* which is most important for our thesis, however, is the negative one—the fact that in *jurisdictio,* unlike *gubernaculum,* the law is something more than a mere directive force. It is not merely the *vis directiva* of St. Thomas, or the moral inhibition implied in the *Digna vox.* Those ought to guide the will of a king and, if he is a good king, they will. But the king may legitimately disregard them, for they are only self-imposed; and, if he refuses to be so guided, he is within his undoubted legal rights in so doing. This is true, however, only within the sphere of government (*gubernaculum*). It is never true in the sphere of jurisdiction, although the king is the sole fountain of justice. For in *jurisdictio,* as contrasted with *gubernaculum,* there are bounds to the king's discretion established by a law that is positive and coercive, and a royal act beyond these bounds is *ultra vires.* It is in *jurisdictio,* therefore, and not in "government" that we find the most striking proof that in medieval England the Roman maxim of absolutism was never in force theoretically or actually. For in jurisdiction the king was bound by his oath to proceed by law and not otherwise. Although the judges were his, appointed by him and acting in his name alone, they were nevertheless bound by their own oaths to determine the rights of the subject not according to the king's will but according to the law; and any careful study of the masses of plea rolls which survive from this period must convince one that this was no mere pious theory, but on the whole the actual and the general practice. When King John substituted his will for this law, in proceeding by force against vassals whose wrong had not been judicially proved, civil war and the Great Charter were the result. The famous thirty-ninth chapter of Magna Carta contains merely the classical statement of a principle that was always insisted upon and usually enforced as a rule of positive coercive law, and not, as the Austinians would say, as a mere maxim of positive morality—the fundamental principle that the king must not take the definition of rights into his own hands, but must proceed against none by force for any alleged violation of them until a case has been made out against such a one by "due process of law."

The two outstanding features that distinguish the medieval constitution from the modern are, then, the separation of government and jurisdiction, and the difference in legal effect between an administrative order and a definition of right. In the seventeenth century, the royalists, citing the undoubted precedents for absolutism in government alone, extended these without warrant into the sphere of mere jurisdiction; while the parliamentarians, seeing the limits of the medieval *jurisdictio,* with equal lack of justification, applied these to acts of government as well as to definitions of right. The mistake was natural, but in a historian it is not therefore the more excusable. In the same way, and for the same reasons, partisans of James I and his son tried to stretch the royal right to issue decrees "annexed" to government, or merely ancillary to jurisdiction, far enough to cover and, in some cases, to trench upon the rights of the subject which a medieval king could not even define without the counsel and consent of his *curia*. The answer to these pretensions made by Sir Edward Coke, constitutionally a medievalist rather than a modern, is an admirable restatement of the ancient doctrine: "The King by his proclamation, or other ways, cannot change any part of the common law, or statute law, or the customs of the realm." [29]

The Roman jurists had distinguished *imperium* and *jurisdictio,* but by the time of Justinian the imperial will completely dominated both, as is proved by Justinian's command to the compilers of the ancient law to make by his sole authority such changes in it as seemed necessary. In medieval England, similar changes might be made lawfully by the king alone in those enactments which he "has within his power" (*habet in potestate sua*), but in none besides. In the field of government proper the absolutist maxim of the *Institutes* truly applied; in *jurisdictio* it had no application whatever. It is on the basis of this distinction between government and law, between Bracton's *gubernaculum* and his *jurisdictio,* that I would venture to try to reconstruct our conception of the medieval constitution, and even of some parts of the modern, for I think they need some reconstructing.

The distinction in question has been illustrated from Bracton, and it is necessary now to show that it persisted after Bracton's age, if it merits the importance I have attributed to it. The most convincing witness I can call to prove this for the end of the middle ages is Sir John Fortescue, Chief Justice of the Court of King's Bench under King Henry VI, whose *Governance of England* has been called the first book to be written in English on the English constitution. The formula for English government which Fortescue offers in almost all his works is contained in his phrase *regimen politicum et regale;* and here his adjective *politicum* applies to Bracton's *jurisdictio,* his *regale* to Bracton's *gubernaculum.* There has been much discussion of this famous phrase, but, so far as I know, the interpretation of it just given was never proposed until I suggested it in 1932. Before then it was customary to identify *regale* with Bracton's *gubernaculum,* but under *politicum* to introduce into both government and jurisdiction the peers who for Bracton have no part in government but only in jurisdiction. Such an interpretation makes of England not a pure monarchy, but a mixed one, if not even somewhat more, a "mixture" of monarchy and republican government, as one eminent authority has put it,[30] rather than the monarchy absolute within certain definite limits established by law, which Bracton certainly implies and, as I believe, Fortescue retains.

The difference between these two conflicting interpretations really lies in the different connotations given to Fortescue's word *politicum.* To the Reverend Charles Plummer that word means "republican"; to me, if I had to choose a single word, it would not mean "republican," but "constitutional." Fortescue's *politicum* does not imply an organ of government responsible to the people and independent of the king, with authority to control his acts of administration—in reality, a mixed and not a pure monarchy—the only possible meaning of the word "republican." Instead, "politicum," in its fifteenth-century use, seems not inconsistent with Bracton's earlier assertion that in government proper the king has no peer, much less a superior. To Fortescue, as to Bracton, it means no more than a negative, legal limit to the king's government, formed by the rights of his subjects which the king has sworn to maintain, and which he cannot lawfully change or blemish or arbitrarily transfer from one to another.

"Republicanism" in the sphere of administration ultimately

became a principle of the English constitution, but it was not for a century and a half after Fortescue's time, and then only as a result of a great civil war. For Sir John Fortescue, as for Bracton, there was and there could be no legitimate government in England except the king's government. What Professor Tout has told us as true of the fourteenth century still remained true in the fifteenth: "The great fact, never to be forgotten, is that the king governed the country and, whatever advice he took, was ultimately responsible for all executive acts." [31]

Fortescue did not say that the government of England was a mere *regimen politicum;* he said it was *regimen politicum et regale.* It was at the same time both "political" and "regal," limited and absolute; and these, for him, were not mutually exclusive terms as they are for us. One of these two interpretations looks forward to the cabinet government of the eighteenth century and afterward, making Fortescue hardly less than a modern; the other looks back to Bracton's description of English institutions as they were about the middle of the thirteenth century, and implies that these institutions survived with little change in fundamentals to the end of the medieval period at least. This is not to overlook or to deny the great constitutional developments between Bracton's day and Fortescue's. When Bracton wrote his great treatise, representatives, so far as we know, had been chosen to attend an English parliament but once, and that for mere participation in a grant of supply; the Commons were as yet no essential part of the national assembly. The enactments which Fortescue has in mind, those which for him make England, unlike France, a true *regimen politicum,* are statutes enacted only by a parliament which, in the words of an English chief justice of the fourteenth century, "represents the body of all the realm." [32] The difference is vast. Yet it remains true, I think, that Fortescue's constitutionalism is medieval and not modern. It still incorporates the essentials of Bracton's theory of the state.

If this interpretation of Fortescue's constitutionalism is the correct one—and I think the subsequent more detailed examination of Mr. S. B. Chrimes [33] has confirmed it—then we must cease to expect to find, and we must give up the assumption that we actually have found, in Fortescue any trace of modern republican or democratic control of national administration. This means that there is nothing in Fortescue's words, or in the political institutions or ideas of the age he describes, of our modern doctrine or practice of "checks and balances." Government, so far as it was strictly government, was then a discretionary power concentrated in a single hand. In 1576 Bodin criticized Aristotle for classifying states on the basis of actual administration, instead of the ultimate source of authority. The hint might apply to medieval constitutionalism as well. No matter how many officials or councils might be employed by a medieval king, if their whole authority was in every case a mere delegation of a royal discretionary power, there is no warrant for our assumption of such anachronisms as mixed monarchy, or "republican" control, or "checks and balances." In the middle ages, as always, there was, of course, the salutary threat of revolution against an oppressive government; but it is a contradiction in terms to call such a check a constitutional or legal one. Within the frame of what we might call the constitution, government proper, as distinguished from *jurisdictio*, was "limited" by no coercive control, but only by the existence beyond it of rights definable by law and not by will.

If such a system had had no great defects, it might have survived to our own day without any supplementary "control" of administration. It is easy enough now to see what the fundamental defect was: it lay in the lack of any effective sanction for these legal limits to arbitrary will. It was not until comparatively modern times that the developments of nationalism and the concentration of national authority convinced men that the principles of the *Digna vox* were not a sufficient protection of liberty and right against arbitrary will. As Professor Tawney says, "Skeptical as to the existence of unicorns and salamanders, the age of Machiavelli and Henry VIII found food for its credulity in the worship of that rare monster, the God-fearing prince." [34]

The addition of the modern political control of government to the medieval legal limitation of it required a revolution— a revolution that reached England only in the seventeenth century, France only at the end of the eighteenth, and cost both countries much blood.

This, however, was a later and a modern development which can be best treated by itself. Meantime, it might be added, the medieval constitutionalism disclosed by the English historical materials was no monopoly of England or of Englishmen, but a *datum* with which the historian must reckon no matter with what particular European constitutional system he is immediately concerned. "Racism" may be a convenient cloak for national aggression, but it is a very inadequate explanation of national constitutional development. A generation or two ago it was the fashion to account for England's unique retention of her medieval constitutionalism by some mysterious quality of the English race or blood, and especially by the Englishman's Germanic strain. Such arguments have now, happily, been left by historians to the propagandists, and they are refuted by the evidences, plentiful and widely scattered, of the existence in many lands of a medieval constitutionalism not essentially unlike England's and, though much more rarely, of the persistence of this constitutionalism to modern times.

The great fourteenth-century jurist, Baldus, in his commentary on Justinian's Code, repeats in general terms the maxim that the prince ought to observe the laws because all his authority comes from them. But the word "ought," he says, must not be taken too literally, because the supreme and absolute power of the prince is not under the law; therefore that law has reference to the ordinary power, not to absolute power (*unde lex ista habet respectum ad potestatem ordinariam non ad potestatem absolutam*).[35] This is a reference to the familiar *merum et mixtum imperium et jurisdictio* with which all continental legal writers of the time are concerned,[36] but the clear distinction of Baldus between a *potestas ordinaria* and a *potestas absoluta* seems to be about the same as Bracton's between *jurisdictio* and *gubernaculum.*

CHAPTER V

The Transition
from Medieval to Modern

AS WE have seen, the fundamental weakness of all medieval constitutionalism lay in its failure to enforce any penalty, except the threat or the exercise of revolutionary force, against a prince who actually trampled under foot those rights of his subjects which undoubtedly lay beyond the scope of his legitimate authority. We must clearly recognize this defect of medieval constitutionalism without denying the existence of the constitutionalism. The importance of the period we are now to consider arises from the attempts then made, and the final success of the attempts, to secure a sanction short of force for these legal rights of the subject against the arbitrary will of the prince.

Looking backward at this struggle one is amazed by its desperate character, the slowness and the lateness of the victory of law over will, the tremendous cost in blood and treasure, and the constitutional revolution required to incorporate the final results in the fabric of modern constitutionalism. Wholly regardless of the respective claims, in the sixteenth century, of protestantism and Catholic orthodoxy, or of those of puritans and their opponents, I think it may be said that had there been no religious schism such as then occurred, a schism unexampled since Roman times in extent and permanence, medieval constitutionalism, with this fatal weakness of its sanctions, might well have been utterly swept away by the rising tide of national power concentrated under the new Renaissance monarchy in a prince who no longer had to defer to the rights and claims of a multitude of powerful feudal lords. The great issue in the sixteenth century was the conflict between the old *gubernaculum* and the old *jurisdictio* over the indefinite line which separated one from the other; and up to the appearance of the religious schism it seemed an unequal struggle in which one outpost of law after another fell before the new forces of despotic will. Throughout the whole range of political literature there is probably no period in which obedience to kings is so stressed as in the first half of the sixteenth century—not even during the reaction in England following the execution of Charles I. In that period, to all appearances, *jurisdictio* was destined to be swallowed up entirely by *gubernaculum;* and if the doctrines of almost unlimited obedience which then prevailed had persisted unchanged, I venture to believe that it would have disappeared.

Among the many surviving examples of these doctrines a single one must suffice here, but this one is the more striking because it comes from William Tyndale, who had suffered much and was to suffer yet more from royal oppression. In 1528 Tyndale wrote in his *Obedience of a Christian Man:*

> For God hath made the kyng in every Realme iudge over all, and over him is there no iudge. He that iudgeth the kyng iudgeth God, and he that layeth handes on the king, layeth hand on God, and he that resisteth the kyng resisteth God, and damneth Gods law and ordinaunce. If the subiectes sinne they must be brought to yᵉ kinges iudgement. If the kyng sinne he must be reserved unto yᵉ iudgement wrath and vengeaunce of God. . . . Hereby seest thou that the kyng is in thys worlde without lawe, and may at his lust doe right or wrong, and shall geve acomptes, but to God onely. . . .

Furthermore though he be the greatest tyraunt in the world, yet is he unto thee a great benefit of God and a thing wherefore thou oughtest to thanke God hyghly . . . when God gave the people of Israell a kyng, it thundred and rained that y⁵ people feared so sore that they cryed to Samuell for to pray for them, that they should not dye. . . . As the law is a terrible thing: even so is the kyng. For he is ordeined to take vengeaunce and hath a sword in his hand and not pecockes feethers. Feare him therfore and looke on hym as thou wouldest looke on a sharpe sword that hangeth ouer thy head by an heare.[1]

It would be difficult to express the theory of royal absolutism in more extreme or more sweeping terms—"the kyng is in thys worlde without lawe." And Tyndale's words did not stand alone.

In the face of this attack, *jurisdictio* was saved from extinction mainly by two things: the unexampled toughness of the ancient English common law and the ultimate emergence of new and radical religious differences among the subjects of the king. The first of these influences has been explained by Maitland in his brilliant Ford Lecture on English Law and the Renaissance. It was in this period that the German reception of Roman law was consummated and there was a serious threat of a similar reception in England. On the political or constitutional side, which mainly concerns us here, what commended the Roman system to its sixteenth-century advocates was not, as to Glanvill or Bracton, its popular origin, but rather its later despotic tendency embodied in the famous maxim: "What has pleased the prince has the force of a *lex*." In any event the Roman attack was a failure, and Maitland has shown how much the inherent strength of the old *jurisdictio* contributed to that result. But the ultimate outcome might well have been vastly different if the strength of the *jurisdictio* had been offset by a government backed by the unanimous support of subjects who continued to think of the king as Tyndale had thought. The fact that it was not so backed we must attribute chiefly to the religious differences which were becoming very grave by the middle of the sixteenth century.

In all the coronation oaths surviving from the middle ages the first and foremost obligation by which the prince is bound is his duty to maintain the Church. Neglect of this duty was considered a misfeasance as serious as injustice, and in the eyes of many religious zealots of the sixteenth century infinitely more serious: the former endangered the immortal souls while the latter endangered merely the bodies of all the king's subjects. In the famous *Vindiciae Contra Tyrannos,* which comes nearest to being the official pronouncement of French Calvinists in the later sixteenth century, the first questions asked and answered are whether a prince's subjects ought to obey if he commands something contrary to the law of God, and whether they may actively resist his attempts to abrogate this law or to "lay waste the Church." Only in the second place is it asked whether a similar resistance is warranted where he is "oppressing the Republic." And Calvin himself had said that "earthly princes when they rise up against God abdicate their authority, nay even become unworthy of being reckoned in the number of men." [2] The effect of religious schism was to give new life and new content to the old theories concerning tyranny. It could scarcely be otherwise under the prevailing conditions, when the king was the vicar of God and defender of the faith, sworn to maintain and enforce religious uniformity throughout a realm in which there was no longer even a semblance of actual uniformity. In such a case it was inevitable that religious groups of every faith, if brought under the king's penalty for nonconformity, should come to regard the ruler not as a true king but as a tyrant, who by fighting against God had abdicated his lawful authority. Boucher, the Catholic *Ligueur,* entitles his book against the king of France *The Just Abdication of Henry III*.[3] Old doctrines of tyranny thus got a new religious content which so weakened respect for all government that the very state was threatened, and eventually a new party was created willing even to tolerate error if such toleration were necessary to save the state from destruction.

In the struggle between *jurisdictio* and *gubernaculum* it was then not merely the toughness of English law that saved it from destruction; it was in part also the weakening of government. The alliance of lawyer and puritan against encroachments of royal power in the later sixteenth and the early seventeenth century is one of the commonplaces of English history, and James I with his practical but shortsighted shrewdness always linked the two together. It is equally significant that he also coupled "puritans and Papists." [4] But here some might question—indeed some have questioned—the very fact of the survival of *jurisdictio* in the Tudor period. The trite and accepted phrase, "Tudor absolutism," seems to imply the contrary, and if it is a wholly correct phrase my premise of the persistence of constitutional limitations must be abandoned. I shall therefore try to indicate a little of the evidence for the survival of *jurisdictio,* and for that of the distinction between it and government. Then I shall turn to the chief contribution of the sixteenth and seventeenth centuries to our modern constitutionalism—the development which culminated in a new political sanction for the old legal limitations on government inherited from the middle ages.

In the transmission to our times of these limitations England's part far outweighs in importance that of any other European country, and this would remain largely true for us even if our peculiar political institutions and ideas were not English in origin. The instinct of Rudolph Gneist was sound when, three-quarters of a century ago, he turned to a study of the English constitution as the basis of his "efforts for reform in the German legal procedure." The history of constitutionalism in the critical sixteenth and seventeenth centuries is therefore mainly a history of some aspects of the English constitution. On the other hand, it would be a serious mistake to assume that these principles of constitutionalism were confined to England alone. For example, the iconoclasm of the French Revolution tended and still tends somewhat to obscure the constitutional principles which were struggling for survival in France under the Old Regime. It may be worth while to look briefly at a few French illustrations of these principles before turning our attention to England.

The word "constitution," as we have seen, acquired its present meaning comparatively lately, but other words were used long before with the same general meaning. As early as 1418 or 1419 Jean de Terre Rouge is certainly thinking of nothing less than a French constitution, and in some sense a fundamental one, when he says: "It is not permissible for the King to change those things which have been ordained *ad statum publicum regni*." [5] Bodin in 1566 entitles the important sixth chapter of his *Methodus,* which deals with constitutional matters, *De statu Rerumpublicarum.* It is with French assertions of this principle in the sixteenth century that we are here concerned, and probably the most definite of them all is the one made by Claude de Seyssell early in the reign of Francis I. "There are, as it were," he says, "three bridles by which the supreme power of the kings of France is restrained": religion, jurisdiction, and *la police.* The third of these consists of the fundamental laws of the monarchy which Jean de Terre Rouge had included within the *status publicus regni*. The second is our ancient *jurisdictio*—the name and the thing, under which Seyssell mentions the *parlements,* constituted, as he says, in order that nothing should be permissible for kings more than has been conceded by law.[6] In 1571 the historian du Haillan repeats these maxims of Seyssell with approval, but confesses with regret that "we retain only the shadow of those good old institutions." [7]

Seyssell's constitutionalism may have been an anachronism, as du Haillan hints, but he spoke as if his principles were still valid, and those principles seem to imply for him nothing less than the fundamentals of a constitution defined by law, unalterable by government, and interpreted by an independent judiciary. The great tradition of constitutionalism can be clearly traced through that unparalleled succession of eminent French jurists and historians from Charles du Moulin in the sixteenth century to Claude Joly in the seventeenth—constitutionalists all, including François Hotman, Bodin, Charondas le Caron, Bacquet, Choppin, du Tillet, du Haillan, Pasquier, De Thou, Coquille, Loyseau, Brisson, the Chancellor De L'Hôpital, La Roche Flavin, Loysel, Lebret, Talon, and many more. By the end of that period French constitutionalism had become even more a shadow than it had been in 1571, but it was the shadow of a substance that we still retain at least in part; and when the great history of constitutionalism comes to be written, it will not be complete without a significant chapter on France under the Old Regime. We must, however, give greater attention to our own earlier institutions, for it was mainly there that the fate of modern constitutionalism was settled. For reasons centering largely in the political institutions peculiar to medieval England, only a few of which can be dealt with in a rapid survey such as this, England was more fortunate than her neighbors in retaining limitations on arbitrary government; and even in England a desperate civil war and a constitutional revolution were finally necessary before adequate sanctions could be found for her medieval constitutionalism. It is on these matters that a survey of the history of constitutionalism must concentrate.

In England, as elsewhere, *jurisdictio* was faced by encroaching government in the sixteenth and seventeenth centuries; yet in England *jurisdictio* had not been overwhelmed by government, and the old line of separation between it and *gubernaculum* was weakened but not destroyed. Constitutional history in this period is chiefly the story of the English attack upon this line and its English defense. Let us look first at the evidence for the survival of *jurisdictio*. Most of it, naturally, is to be found in the law reports of the period, but some of the letters of Stephen Gardiner, chancellor of England in the reign of Queen Mary, seem almost as significant. In 1547 Gardiner wrote thus to the Privy Council:

And thus I have hard the lerned men of the Common Law say that if any, althogh he be deputed by the King, do, in execution of spirituall jurisdiction, extend the same contrary to any Common Law or act of Parliament, it is a premunire both to the judge and the parties, althogh it be done in the Kings Majesties name; bicause they say the Kinges Majesties supremacie in visiting and ordring of the Churche is reserved to spirituall jurisdiction. Which their saing cold not sinke into my understanding, that men executing the Kings commission, and having of hym jurisdiction, cold faull in danger of a premunire. But so the best lerned men of the realme have said, and I wold fayne have persuaded them to the contrary.[8]

In another letter of the same year Gardiner said:

100

And of what strenkythe an acte of Parliament is, the realme was taught in the case of her that we called Quene Anne; where all suche as spake ageynst her in the Parliament House, all though they ded it by speciall commaundement of the Kynge, and spake that was truth, yet they were fayne to have a pardon, by cause that speakinge was ageynst an acte of Parliament. Ded ye never knowe or here tell of any man, that for doynge that the Kynge our late sovereigne lorde willed, devysed, and requyred to be done, he that tooke paynes and was commaunded to do it, was fayne to sue for his pardon, and suche other allso as were doers in it? And I coulde tell who it were. Sure there hathe bene suche a case; and I have bene present when it hathe bene reasoned that the doinge ageynst an acte of Parliament excusethe not a man even from the case of treason, all thoughe a man ded it by the Kynges commaundement. Ye can call this to your rememberance, when ye thinke furder of it; and when it comythe to your rememberaunce, ye will not be best content with your selfe, I beleve, to have advysed me to entre the breache of an acte of Parliament, withoute suertie of pardon, all thoughe the Kynge commaunded it.[9]

In Gardiner's long letter written from the Fleet prison to the Protector Somerset in 1547 [10] several well-known but remarkable passages occur which I am loth to omit as illustrations, both of the strength of the old *jurisdictio,* and of Gardiner's apparent dislike of it. It is a very human document. He refers to the authority of papal legate which Wolsey had obtained with Henry VIII's full knowledge and at his express request. "Yet," Gardiner says, "because it was agaynst the lawes of the realme, the judges concluded the offence of the premunire; which conclusyion I bare away, and take it for a law of the realme, because the lawyers so sayd, but my resone digested it not." In support of this decision, Gardiner says that the lawyers brought in examples of many judges that had fines set on their heads in like cases for doing against the lawes of the realme by the Kings commaundement. And then was brought in the judges oth, not to staye any process or judgement for any commaundement from the Kinges Majesty. And one article agaynst my Lord Cardinal was that he had graunted injunctions to stay the Common Lawes. And upon that occasion *Magna Charta* was spoken of, and it was made a great matter, the stay of the Common Lawe. And this I lerned in that case.

Gardiner then refers to his experience of enactments of the Council against exporters of grain, ineffective because "at such thime as the transgressors should be ponished, the judges whould answere, it might not be by the lawes"; and to the famous Act of Proclamations of 1539, "in the passing of which act many liberall wordes were spoken, and a playne promes that, by autority of the Act for Proclamationes, nothing should be made contrary to an act of Parliament or Common Law." He recalls one case in which he argued with Audley, the chancellor, against inflicting the penalties of the Statute of Praemunire, and then quotes Audley's answer as follows:

"Thou art a good felow, Bishop," quod he (which was the maner of his familier speach), "looke the Act of Supremacy, and there the Kings doinges be restrayned to spiritual jurisdiction; and in a nother acte it is provided that no Spirituall Lawe shall have place contrary to a Common Lawe or Acte of Parliament. And this were not," quod he, "you bishops would enter in with the Kinge and, by meanes of his supremacie, order the layty as ye listed. But we will provide," quod he, "that the premunire shall ever hang over your heads, and so we lay men shal be sure to enjoye our inheritaunce by the Common Lawes and acts of Parliament."

102

Finally Gardiner recounts an episode of Henry VIII's reign which furnishes probably the clearest of the proofs of his own defensive thesis and of several of mine.

The Lord Cromwell had once put in the Kinges our late sovereigne lordes head to take upon him to have his will and pleasure regarded for a lawe; for that, he sayd, was to be a very kinge. And therupon I was called for at Hampton Court. And as the Lord Cromwell was very stout, "Come on my Lord of Winchester," quod he (for that conceat he had, what so ever he talked with me, he knewe ever as much as I, Greke or Laten and all), "Aunswer the King here," quod he, "but speake plainly and direccly, and shrink not, man! Is not that," quod he, "that pleaseth the King, a lawe? Have ye not ther in the Civill Lawe," quod he, "*quod principi placuit,* and so fourth?" quod he, "I have somwhat forgotten it now." I stode still and woundred in my mind to what conclusion this should tend. The King sawe me musing, and with ernest gentelnes sayd, "Aunswere him whether it be so or no." I would not aunswere my Lord Cromewell, but delivered my speache to the King, and tolde him I had red in dede of kings that had there will alwayes receaved for a lawe, but, I told him, the forme of his reigne, to make the lawes his wil, was more sure and quiet. "And by thys forme of goverment ye be established," quod I, "and it is agreable with the nature of your people. If ye begin a new maner of policye, how it will frame, no man can tell; and how this frameth ye can tell; and I would never advise your Grace to leave a certeine for an uncerteine." The King turned his back and left the matter after.

A dozen years later than this, in the first year of Elizabeth, John Aylmer, later bishop of London, wrote his *Harborough for All Faithfull and Trewe Subjects* in answer to John Knox's *First Blast of the Trumpet Against the Monstruous Regiment of Women.* It contains a statement of constitutionalism hardly less striking than Gardiner's:

103

The regemente of Englande is not a mere monarchie, as some for lacke of consideracion thinke, nor a mere oligarchie nor democracie, but a rule mixed of all these, wherein ech one of these have or should have like authoritie. The image whereof, and not the image, but the thinge indede, is to be sene in the parliament hous, wherein you shall find these 3 estats; the king or quene which representeth the monarche, the noblemen which be the aristocratie, and the burgesses and knights the democratcie. . . . If the parliament use their privileges, the king can ordain nothing without them: If he do it, it is his fault in usurping it, and their fault in permitting it. Wherefore, in my judgment, those that in King Henry the VIII.'s daies would not grant him that his proclamations should have the force of a statute, were good fathers of the countrie, and worthy commendacion in defending their liberty. . . .

But to what purpose is all this? To declare that it is not in England so daungerous a matter to have a woman ruler, as men take it to be. . . . If, on thother part, the regiment were such as all hanged upon the king's or quene's wil, and not upon the lawes written; if she might decre and make lawes alone, without her senate; if she judged offences according to her wisdom, and not by limitation of statutes and laws; if she might dispose alone of war and peace; if, to be short, she wer a mer monarch, and not a mixed ruler, you might peradventure make me fear the matter the more, and the less to defend the cause.[11]

This statement is remarkable in more ways than one for a date so early as 1559; it includes not only an unequivocal statement of our ancient legal limitations on the prince's authority, but an assertion—one of the earliest I have met with—of mixed monarchy as the true form of the English government. In addition, it places matters of peace and war within the powers of parliament instead of the king alone—a principle that, so far as I know, was never seriously urged in parliament till 1621, and was then repudiated by the king.

104

That Aylmer's assertion above is true, that in England all did not hang upon the queen's will, but "upon the lawes written," we find ample proof in the law reports of the time. Thus we find in Judge Jenkins' summaries of cases in the Exchequer Chamber: "The King by his grant cannot exclude himself from prosecuting any plea of the Crown; for it concerns the publick Government, and cannot be separated from his person." [12] "Where the King has an Estate in fee or for life in any land, the king's grant of it *quamdiu in manibus nostris fore contigerit*, is a void grant; for such a grant was never heard of." [13] "The King cannot grant to any one a power to dispence with any penal statute." [14] "The King cannot grant power to any to make justices of oyer and terminer." [15] "Regularly the King is only subject to the law of nature, as to the rights of the Crown; as to the rights of the subject he is bounded by the laws of the land." [16] But the clearest of all such cases is that of Cavendish in 1587, when the justices of the Court of Common Pleas flatly refused to obey express and repeated orders of the Queen, on the ground that "the orders were against the law of the land, in which case it was said, no one is bound to obey such an order." [17]

A half-dozen years later, when Serjeant Heyle ventured to say in the House of Commons that the queen "hath as much right to all our Lands and Goods as to any Revenue of her Crown," D'Ewes says, "All the House hemm'd and laughed and talked." [18] It may have been similar opinions expressed in the same parliament by an unnamed "old Doctor of the Civil Law," on hearing of which D'Ewes says, "The House hawk'd and spat and kept a great coil to make him make an end." [19]

These were rights of the subject protected by due process of law; but over against them was the king's government in which he was "subject only to the law of nature." We might

105

offset Aylmer's constitutionalism by a statement attributed by Thomas Starkey to Cardinal Pole in the supposed dialogue between Pole and Lupset:

Hyt ys not unknown to you, Master Lupset, that our cuntrey hathe byn governyd and rulyd thes many yerys under the state of pryncys, wych by theyr regal powar and pryncely authoryte, have jugyd al thingys perteynyng to the state of our reame to hange only upon theyr wyl and fantasye; insomuch that, what so ever they ever have conceyvyd or purposyd in theyr myndys, they thought, by and by, to have hyt put in effecte, wythout resystens to be made by any private man and subyecte; or else, by and by, they have sayd that men schold mynysch theyr pryncely authoryte. For what ys a prynce (as hyt ys commynly sayd) but he may dow what he wyl? Hyt ys thought that al holly hangyth apon hys only arbytryment. Thys hath byn thought, ye, and thys yet ys thought, to perteyne to the maiesty of a prynce—to moderate and rule al thyng accordyng to hys wyl and plesure; wych ys, wythout dowte, and ever hath byn, the gretyst destructyon to thys reame, ye, and to al other, that ever hathe come therto.[20]

If Gardiner does not misrepresent him, these were precisely the opinions of Thomas Cromwell: to be a "very king" the prince must make his will a law. It seems probable that the dialogue of Cromwell and Gardiner at Hampton Court, referred to in Gardiner's letter to Somerset, was the prelude to Henry's attempt to put in practice this conception of kingship of Cromwell's by the Statute of Proclamations in 1539. It seems equally likely that Aylmer's praise of "the good fathers of the country" had reference to the men in the House of Commons who forced the king to substitute for his original bill a new one which specifically excepted from the king's proclamations the "inheritances, lawful possessions, offices, liberties, privileges, franchises, goods, or chattels" of subjects, and forbade the infringement of any "acts, common laws, . . . [or] lawful and laudable customs" of the realm. It may have been these things that Starkey also had in mind.[21]

Clearly a struggle was going on in England between will and law about the year 1539, and it was to last for one hundred and fifty years. That it did not reach the phase of open warfare before the Stuarts is to be explained chiefly by the nature of parliament in the Tudor period. "It is of interest to note," says Professor Cheyney,

that the queen [Elizabeth] used the expressions "this parliament" and "parliaments," as indeed was practically universal contemporary usage. She hardly conceived of "parliament" as a permanent institution. There was not in her view a coördinate branch of government known as parliament; rather from time to time a special assembly known as a parliament was called. The permanent continuous government was the queen, her privy councillors, judges and other officials.[22]

Sir Thomas Smith in his *De Republica Anglorum*, written in Elizabeth's reign, devotes considerable space to parliament; and yet, I believe, the statement of Sir John Seeley was on the whole a true one when he said that "in Queen Elizabeth's reign it would not have been natural . . . in describing the government of England to mention Parliament at all. Not exactly that Parliament was subservient, but, that, in general Parliament was not there." [23]

In the forty-five years of Elizabeth's reign there were only eleven parliaments, whose duration was seldom longer than a few weeks; and I think one must agree with the further conclusion of Sir John Seeley, that the beginnings of parliament as a normal and regular organ of English government are to be found only after the Restoration. That, he says, "is the epoch from which we may say that *the permanence of Parliament* dates." [24] Even in the comparatively short periods when parliament was in session the influence of the king was predominant and the "absolute" character of his government was recognized by the parliament itself. The words of Henry VIII in Ferrer's Case were indicative of the facts when he said: "We at no time stand so high in our estate royal as in the time of parliament; when we as head and you as members are conjoined and knit together into one body politic." [25] It was never forgotten, by king or parliament, that the king was the real head; and in 1535 Stephen Gardiner held in his *Oratio de Vera Obedientia* that this was a headship in matters ecclesiastical as temporal:

seeinge the churche of Englande consisteth of the same sortes of people at this daye that are comprised in this worde realme of whom the kinge his called the headde: Shall he not beinge called the headde of the realme of Englande be also the headde of the same men whan they are named the churche of Englande? [26]

In all these matters of government proper, and not of mere *jurisdictio,* the debates of Elizabeth's parliaments collected by Sir Simonds D'Ewes furnish concrete and conclusive evidence that the paramount and unquestioned authority of the prince as head was fully recognized and accepted by parliament itself—evidence which is all the more significant when we contrast it with the strenuous and successful opposition offered by parliament when Henry VIII attempted to invade the sphere of jurisdiction in the Statute of Proclamations.

Interesting examples of the insistence by the queen, and at times of the clear acknowledgment by parliament, that government proper was not parliament's province, but that of the prince alone, occur in almost every one of Elizabeth's parliaments from 1566 on. I have time to note only a few. In 1559, in the very first parliament of the reign, Sir Nicholas Bacon, the lord keeper, warned the members that they should

clearly forbear, and, as a great enemy to good Council, fly from all manner of Contentions, Reasonings, Disputations, and all Sophistical Captious and frivolous Arguments and Quiddities, meeter for ostentation of Wit, than Consultation of weighty Matters, comelier for Scholars than Counsellors; more beseeming for Schools, than for Parliament Houses.[27]

Not bad advice to any legislative body, but rather ominous coming from such a source. And at the end of the parliament of 1571 the lord keeper reproved certain of the members,

although not many in number, who in the proceeding of this Session, have shewed themselves audacious, arrogant, and presumptuous, calling her Majesties Grants and Prerogatives also in question, contrary to their duty and place that they be called unto; and contrary to the express Admonition given in her Majesties name, in the beginning of this Parliament.

These, he says, her Majesty condemns "for their audacious, arrogant and presumptuous folly, thus by superfluous speech spending much time in medling with matters neither pertaining to them nor within the capacity of their understanding." [28] In the same session the speaker of the Commons himself admitted that in matters ecclesiastical "wholly her Majesties Power is absolute"; [29] and one member, for encroaching upon this power by proposing a bill for reforming the ceremonies of the Church, was called before the Privy Council and commanded meantime to remain away from the parliament.[30] Exhibiting such a bill, the treasurer declared, was "against the Prerogative of the Queen, which was not to be tolerated." The prerogative in this respect was, as one member put it, "not disputable." [31] And the queen herself sent word to the Commons that she "would not suffer these things to be Ordered by Parliament." [32]

The boldness of Strickland, who was thus sequestered by the council in 1571 was, however, exceeded in the speech of Peter Wentworth in the parliament of 1575, for which the Treasurer

moved for his punishment and Imprisonment in the Tower as the House should think good and consider of; whereupon after sundry Disputations and Speeches, it was ordered upon the Question, that the said Peter Wentworth should be committed close Prisoner to the Tower for his said offence, there to remain until such time as this House should have further Consideration of him.[33]

When the Commons in the parliament of 1580 had ventured to pass Paul Wentworth's resolution for a public fast day "without her Majesty's Privity and Pleasure first known," they were rebuked and compelled to make humble submission to the queen for thus daring to "intrude upon her Authority Ecclesiastical"; and when one member rose to protest, the speaker and the House, as D'Ewes says, "did stay him." [34] At the opening of the session of 1593 the lord keeper, "having received new instructions from the Queen," closed his address to the parliament with these notable words:

Wherefore, Mr. Speaker, her Majesties Pleasure is, that if you perceive any idle Heads which will not stick to hazard their own Estates, which will meddle with reforming the Church *and transforming the Commonwealth,* and do exhibit any Bills to such purpose, that you receive them not, until they be viewed and considered by those, who it is fitter should consider of such things, and can better judge of them.[35]

Later, when a bill was drawn by Peter Wentworth and another

"for entailing the Succession of the Crown," the delinquents were called before the council, which commanded them "to forbear the Parliament, and not to go out from their several Lodgings." [36]

It seems reasonably certain that the line so clearly drawn by Bracton between *jurisdictio* and *gubernaculum* in the thirteenth century still remains at the end of the sixteenth the main clue to the riddle of the English constitution. At the close of Elizabeth's reign, with only a few exceptions men seemed to accept, almost as fully as Bracton, the twofold theory that the king is under the law and yet under no man, that private right is determinable and enforceable by law, and is under the control of courts and parliaments; while "matters of state," or the "transforming of the Commonwealth," are things "neither pertaining to them nor within the capacity of their understanding." The latter are a part of "the Prerogative Imperial," [37] which is and ought to be "absolute" and "not disputable." But this delicate balance between jurisdiction and government could only be kept if the head and the members of the commonwealth remained "conjoined and knit together into one body politic," as Henry VIII said. The seams joining them were beginning to show signs of strain even in the reign of Elizabeth; and under her successor rents began to appear, which were soon to widen till the state was divided. A declaration of Sir Walter Raleigh's is significant:

If the House press the King to grant unto them all that is theirs by the law, they cannot in justice refuse the King all that is his by the law. And where will be the issue of such a contention? I dare not divine; but sure I am that it will tend to the prejudice both of King and subject.[38]

These were prophetic words.

111

In the contention between *jurisdictio* and *gubernaculum* which was becoming imminent in the later years of Elizabeth's reign and developed into an open strife under her successor, each side emphasized the fact that its rights were an "inheritance." The parliament itself unwittingly strengthened the position of James I in the first statute of his reign when they declared, in the face of a statute of Henry VIII still in force and flatly contrary, that

the Imperial Crown of the realm of England, and of all the kingdoms, dominions, and rights belonging to the same, did by inherent birthright and lawful and undoubted succession descend and come to your most excellent Majesty, as being lineally, justly, and lawfully next and sole heir of the blood royal of this realm.[39]

James himself always insisted on his royal rights as an inheritance. To him the "fundamental" laws, if any were fundamental, gave protection, not to the subject, but to him alone; they were "onely those Lawes whereby confusion is avoyded, and their King's descent mainteined, and the heritage of the succession and Monarchie." [40] They were no part of the common law, and therefore "not fit for the tongue of any lawyer" even in the high court of parliament. That "highest and most authenticall court of Englande," as Sir Thomas Smith had called it,[41] was itself for James merely a "subalterin iudiciall seate." [42] Like the parliament of Scotland where the members "must not speake without the Chauncellors leave," it was no place "for every rash and hare-brained fellow to propone new Lawes of his owne invention." [43] As late as 1621 he ordered the speaker of the Commons "to acquaint that house with our pleasure, that none therein shall presume to meddle with anything concerning our government or mysteries of state," and to warn them

that we think ourself very free and able to punish any man's mis-
demeanours in parl. as well as during their sitting as after. . . .[44]

We cannot allow of the stile, calling it [parliamentary privilege]
your antient and undoubted right and inheritance, but could rather
have wished that ye had said, that your privileges were derived
from the grace and permission of our ancestors and us; (for most
of them grow from precedents, which shews rather a toleration
than inheritance). . . . So as your house shall only have need to
beware to trench upon the prerogative of the crown; which would
enforce us, or any just king, to retrench them of their privileges,
that would pare his prerogative and flowers of the crown.[45]

"The plain truth is," as he said later, "that we cannot, with
patience, endure our subjects to use such antimonarchical
words to us, concerning their liberties, except they had sub-
joined that they were granted unto them by the grace and
favour of our predecessors." [46]

The true nature and the gravity of this issue are indicated in
the replies to these assertions of the king, made by such men
as Sir Thomas Wentworth, later earl of Strafford and Sir
Edward Coke. In one of the newly discovered diaries of this
parliament of 1621 Wentworth is reported to have said, "The
common Lawes are but custome, and wee claime our liberties
by the same title as we doe our estates, by custome." [47] The
crisis of the constitution, and of constitutionalism, could hardly
have been expressed in fewer or truer words, and Coke's are
equally significant: "When the kinge sayes he can not allowe
our liberties of right, this strikes at the roote. Wee serve here
for thousands and tenn thousands." [48] This was a life-and-
death struggle between liberties held "of right," as the subject's estates were, and James's view that they were "derived
from the grace and permission of our ancestors and us"; it was

113

a dramatic collision of the old *jurisdictio* and *gubernaculum.*

The liberties of the people were to them as much an inheritance guaranteed by the common law as the hereditary right to his authority, independent of that law, was to James; and in a case of the third year of Elizabeth it had been asserted in the court of Common Pleas that, since a particular statute had been enacted

to save Men's Inheritance, we ought to construe it according to the Consideration of the Common Law, and to admeasure the Prerogatives of the King upon this Act, which is made for the Safety of the Inheritances of others, in such Manner as the Common Law admeasures them in Cases that affect the Inheritances of others at Common Law. . . . The King's Prerogative by the Common Law cannot prevail against such a custom as stands with the Right of Inheritance of another.

In case of a procedure where "the Party might be disinherited thereby . . . the Common Law will not suffer the King to have such a Prerogative." Therefore it was said that the king was bound by the statute in question,

for of a Law which belongs to a common Person, be it the Common Law or a special Law, every Man shall take advantage, which the King of common Right cannot defeat, for every Man is an Inheritor to this Common Law of Addition as well as to any other Common Law, which the King cannot defeat without Parliament, for of this Law every Man shall take advantage. . . . Every Subject may claim from him Justice and the King is forced by Justice to do that which he ought.[49]

The wily king had hinted that the privileges of parliament depended solely on precedents. He might have taken warning from Coke's reply, that the Commons "served for thousands and tens of thousands," or from Wentworth's earlier statement:

"We are they that represent the great bulk of the common-wealth." [50] For in these replies we find the first vague promise of the future constitutional principle of the responsibility of government to the people, as a matter not merely of law but of policy. The crisis of 1621 is one of the turning points in the history of constitutionalism. It marks the coming of the new principle of political responsibility to reinforce the old guarantee of law, for the protection of the rights of the subject when threatened by arbitrary will. Parliament was not merely "the most authenticall court" for the determination of private right; it was that, but it was more. It represented "the great bulk of the Commonwealth," and was now beginning to act in their name and in their interest against a "head" whose hereditary rights could no longer be reconciled with the traditional liberties of the members of the commonwealth.

This principle of the people's consent and of parliament as the channel of this consent, reasserted by Wentworth and Coke in 1621, is a very ancient one. As we have seen, it was the original foundation of the binding force of *leges* in republican Rome; [51] and it was asserted by Bracton in his repetition of Papinian's dictum that *lex* is the "common engagement" of the republic,[52] and in his *Introductio* when he said that laws could "neither be changed nor destroyed without the common consent of all those with whose counsel and consent they have been promulgated." [53] This is the principle to which Edward I referred in his summonses to the parliament of 1295—*quod omnes tangit ab omnibus approbetur.*[54] It is also implied in the repudiation by parliament in 1366 of the papal overlordship of England and Ireland because neither King John who had conceded it, nor any other, could place his realm or his people under such subjection "without their assent and agreement." [55]

The general principle is ancient and is clear; but it was long before the corollary became equally clear—that the voice of parliament is the voice of the people. As late as 1365 counsel was arguing in an English court that one accused of breach of a statute could not be guilty if the statute had not been proclaimed locally in his county; [56] as late as 1441 it was seriously debated in the courts whether a churchman's subsequent vote in Convocation should estop him from claiming an immunity granted by royal charter, thus implying that an act of Convocation is merely the act of its members individually; [57] and as late as 1550 the following words were used by the chief justice of the court of Common Pleas to explain the effect of the recent Statute of Uses:

And when the Statute 27 H 8 was made, it gave the land to them that had the use. It is to be seen then, who shall be adjudged in Law the Donor after the Execution of the Possession to the Use. And, Sir, the Parliament (which is nothing but a Court) may not be adjudged the Donor. For what the Parliament did was only a Conveyance . . . from one to another, and a Conveyance by Parliament does not make the Parliament Donor; but it seems to me that Feoffees to Use shall be the Donors, for when a Gift is made by Parliament, every Person in the Realm is privy to it, and assents to it, but yet the Thing shall pass from him that has the most Right and Authority to give it. . . . So here it shall be said the Gift of the Feoffees by Parliament, and the Assent and Confirmation of all others. For if it should be adjudged the Gift of any other, then the Parliament would do a Wrong to the Feoffees in taking a thing from them, and making another the Donor of it.[58]

By some such fiction as this the Roman *lex* had been transformed, and it now furnished a basis for the beginnings of a new theory of parliamentary sovereignty; for its underlying assumption of consent and representation concealed the extent of parliament's potential control over individual right.[59] Wentworth was speaking the language of the future when he said, "We are they that represent the great bulk of the commonwealth"; of the past, when he appealed to custom as the subjects' title to liberty and property. But in 1621 both right and representation were threatened by the rapid extension of royal power.

The old dichotomy of jurisdiction and government was now strikingly displaying its one essential weakness—the lack of sanction for the protection of the sphere of law from invasion by the power of government. To a careful reader of the great constitutional law cases of the Stuart period nothing is more obvious than the embarrassment and hesitancy of the great defenders of individual liberty, such as Selden and Hakewill. If they were not to proclaim themselves revolutionists, which no man dreamt of doing or dared to do before the Long Parliament, these men had no recourse but to rely on earlier precedents; and these precedents afforded very inadequate protection for the rights they recognized. What was needed was a penalty for breaches of right, and there was none. Nothing less than a revolution could add the sanction necessary to make the people's legal liberties secure, but men were not yet ready openly to preach revolution. James had shown his accustomed shrewdness by relying on precedent in his argument against parliamentary privilege; for precedent clearly recognized the power of the king as absolute in government, and it provided no adequate check for an abuse or undue extension of the king's discretionary power beyond its legitimate sphere.

Discretionary powers are by their very definition not controllable by any law. It is as true now as in 1621. Under the pardoning power a governor of one of our states can make gaol delivery of all the dangerous criminals in its prisons, and it is not so long since something like that was actually done.

Jurisdictio marked the limits of the king's authority but provided no means of enforcing their observance. One practical difficulty lay in the very indistinctness of the line dividing the spheres of royal government and private right and the ease with which that line might be ignored by the king on the pretext of "reasons of state" or the familiar and ever-present excuse of "national emergency." An interesting instance of this dangerous indefiniteness, and one concerned with the personal rather than the proprietary rights of the subject, is afforded by the history of judicial torture in England. Torture, Sir Thomas Smith piously declared, "is not used in England, it is taken for servile." [60] "The nature of our nation is free, stout, haulte, prodigall of life and bloud: but contumelie, beatings, servitude and servile torment and punishment it will not abide." [61] "Heading, tormenting, dismembring, either arme or legge, breaking upon the wheele, empailing, and suche cruell torments as be used in other nations by the order of their law, we have not." [62] "There is no one opinion in our Books, or judiciall Record (that we have seen and remember) for the maintenance of tortures or torments, &c.," says Sir Edward Coke in his *Third Institute*.[63]

And yet the actual occurrence of such "cruell torments" in England in the reigns of Elizabeth and James I is attested by evidence that is unquestionable.[64] "Torture was constantly used as an instrument of evidence in the investigation of offences, whether municipal or political, without scruple, and without question as to its legality." [65] In the case of Peacham in 1615 Secretary Winwood reported, "Upon these interrogatories Peacham this day was examined before torture, in torture, between torture and after torture." [66] In 1571, only a few years after writing the statement above that torture was "not used in England," Sir Thomas Smith wrote to Burleigh concerning prisoners implicated in the treason of the duke of Norfolk, "Tomorrow do we intend to bring a couple of them to the rack." [67] The queen had commanded that they should "find the tast therof," [68] and they probably did. Coke himself, when attorney general, seems to have authorized the use of torture on at least one occasion.[69]

This anomaly has often been attributed to the mere weakness or cowardice of the officials involved—an explanation no more satisfactory than the usual indiscriminate condemnation of all the king's judges of the time; while Francis Hargrave thought that the instances of torture proved nothing more than "an irregularity of practice." [70] The true and, to me, the only adequate explanation of these many instances is given by Jardine, to whom they "show, not the casual, capricious, or unjust acts of particular kings or councillors, but a practice handed down and justified by a constant course of precedents as an unquestionable prerogative of the Crown, though directly opposed to the fundamental principles of reason and law." "No doubt," he says,

the assertion of the illegality of torture is in one sense strictly true. It was *not* lawful by the common law; . . . it was contrary to Magna Charta and many statutes; and therefore the Judges could not inflict it as a punishment in the ordinary course of administering justice. But it *was* lawful as an act of prerogative,—as an act of that power to which, according to the doctrines of those days, the laws belonged as a kind of property,—a power, which was superior to the laws, and was able to suspend the laws,—and which was the only and uncontrolled tribunal to judge of the necessity of such suspension.[71]

As Gardiner briefly puts it, "Torture had been allowed by custom as inflicted by prerogative, but not by law." [72] "Here in England, they take a man & rack him I doe not know why, nor

119

when, not in time of Judicature, but when some body bidds,"
says the caustic Selden.[73] The rack is thus only another case,
and one very dangerous to liberty, of the old parallelism of
jurisdictio and government. The king's prerogative in this
matter was not merely "out of the course of the common law,"
as Blackstone said in the next century; it was still in danger of
being "above" it, as Dr. Cowell, in his *Interpreter,* said it was
in 1607.

What was thus true of secular cases before the council was
equally true of ecclesiastical cases coming under the High
Commission. The oath *Ex Officio,* which required one accused
of nonconformity to incriminate himself under oath, was a
procedure flatly contrary to common law and never employed in a common-law court, but its use was common in the
prerogative court of the High Commission for Ecclesiastical
Causes.[74]

Other illustrations of the relations of government to law in
the critical period of constitutionalism about the opening of
the seventeenth century might easily be added,[75] but of them
all royal monopolies are in some ways the most striking. For
such a monopoly was by definition a branch of the prerogative
in the hands of a subject. It originated in a grant made by virtue of the king's "absolute" authority as "supreme governor,"
and in the eye of the monarch was therefore not controllable
by any law nor debatable by subjects even in the high court
of parliament. It was, as Elizabeth said in 1597, if Egerton reported her correctly, "the chiefest Flower in her Garden, and
the principal and head Pearl in her Crown and Diadem." [76]
On the other hand, these monopolies were often clearly against
both statute and common law as well as oppressive in their
actual effects. Did they therefore come within the "absolute"
powers of the prince as mere "matter of polity," or were they

subject to the rules of the law, enforceable by the courts? This
was the constitutional question, and it was a question of first
importance both practical and theoretical.

Up to a year or two before her death Elizabeth had no doubt
about the answer. Monopolies were her concern alone. She
certainly thought them not "fit for the tongue of any lawyer."
As late as October 7, 1601, when a plaintiff tried to bring in
question the legality of Darcy's monopoly of the manufacture
of playing cards by an action in the Common Pleas, the council
at the queen's instance issued an order to the justices of that
court commanding them to stay all proceedings till the queen's
pleasure was made known to them. "Her Prerogative Royall
may not be called in question for the valliditie of the letters
patentes." [77] In 1603 this very patent was declared to be
against law in the case of Darcy v. Allen.[78] But in the meantime, some six weeks after the council's order just mentioned,
the House of Commons took up the question of monopolies in
a five days' debate which is without parallel in the surviving
records of earlier parliamentary history. A list was read of the
new patents granted since the last parliament. "Is not Bread
there?" asked William Hakewill. "If order be not taken for
these, Bread will be there, before the next Parliament." [79]
Despite the strenuous efforts of the ministers, who urged a
procedure by humble petition to the queen, it was evident
that the house was resolved on the bold step of proceeding by
bill to restrict the royal prerogative—a method without precedent. In the accusations against Richard II parliament had
charged the king with saying that the laws were "in his mouth."
Here was a proceeding on the part of parliament which, when
Elizabeth first came to the throne, would have seemed hardly
less revolutionary than the assertions of Richard II. The
speaker was summoned to the queen in haste on November

24, 1601, while the debate was at its height, and the next day announced to the house a message from Elizabeth promising full redress of all their grievances not *in futuro* but at once. "What patent soever is granted," Secretary Cecil added, "there shall be left to the overthrow of that Patent, a Liberty agreeable to the Law." [80] Three days later the Queen was as good as her word and issued a proclamation "by her regal power and authority" and of "her mere grace and favor," in which some monopolies were abolished and most of the others "left to law," adding, however, "that if any of her subjects shall seditiously or contemptuously presume to call in question the power or validity of her prerogative royal, annexed to her imperial crown, in such cases all such persons so offending shall receive severe punishment, according to their demerits." [81] It was a virtual surrender that these last words hardly served to conceal.

The threat against law and jurisdiction and against all legal rights, inherent in a prerogative with boundaries as vague and ill-defined as Elizabeth's, was made evident to Englishmen probably far more by the greed of the holders of royal patents than by any oppressive acts of direct government on the part of the queen herself. What uncertainty was left in 1603, however, the first two Stuarts proceeded without much delay to remove.

CHAPTER VI

Modern Constitutionalism
and Its Problems

IF THE historic evolution of modern constitutionalism is to be made explicable there remain, I take it, at least three major topics to be discussed: first, the views concerning it which seemed to prevail in Stuart England before the struggle for actual supremacy overshadowed all arguments based upon right or constitutional precedent; secondly, the growth of the conviction, toward the end of this period, that existing law was no sufficient guarantee of the liberty of the subject without the addition of sanctions which no constitutional precedents before 1603 adequately gave; and, lastly, the constitutional problems of the modern world which have resulted from the establishment of such sanctions by making the governor responsible to the law and, politically, to the governed.

Briefly stated, the constitutional views in the opening years of the Stuart regime do not seem essentially different from those of the Tudor period. What the Venetian ambassador reported of England in the year 1551 remained substantially true immediately after 1603: "The King of England exercises two powers; . . . the one royal and absolute, the other ordinary and legal." [1] This view was never put more clearly than by Baron Fleming when, in 1606, he gave judgment for the king in the great case of Bate, speaking as follows:

123

And first, for the person of the King, "omnis potestas a Deo, et non est potestas nisi pro bono." To the King is committed the government of the realm and his people; and Bracton saith, that for his discharge of his office, God had given him power, the act of government, and the power to govern. The King's power is double, *ordinary and absolute,* and they have several lawes and ends. That of the ordinary is for the profit of particular subjects, for the execution of civil justice, and the determining of *meum;* and this is exercised by equitie and justice in ordinary courts, and by the civilians is nominated *jus privatum* and with us, common law; and these laws cannot be changed, without parliament; and although that their form and course may be changed and interrupted, yet they can never be changed in substance. The absolute power of the King is not that which is converted or executed to private use, to the benefit of any particular person, but is only that which is applied to the general benefit of the people, and is *salus populi;* as the people is the body and the King the head; and this power is guided by the rules, which direct only at the common law, and is most properly named *Pollicy and Government;* and as the constitution of this body varieth with the same, so varieth this absolute law, *according to the wisdome of the King,* for the *common* good; and these being general rules and true as they are, *all things done within these rules are lawful.* The matter in question [levying an import duty on currants by mere royal proclamation without sanction of an Act of Parliament] is *material matter of state,* and ought to be ruled *by the rules of pollicy;* and if it be so, the King hath done well to execute his extraordinary power.[2]

Other instances of the same view might be given almost without number, and before 1627 we find it asserted at times even by the men who in later years were to be its most strenuous opponents. As late as 1621 Sir Edward Coke himself admitted that there was a prerogative "indisputable." [3] Sir Edward Crawley in the ship-money case contrasted this with the ordinary or "disputable" prerogative by calling it "regal" in distinction from "legal." [4] James I spoke of it as his "public prerogative," or "mystery of state," the *arcanum imperii,* "not fit for the tongue of any lawyer," while he professed that in his "private prerogative" he was always willing to submit to the judgment of the courts.[5] Hobbes had the same distinction in mind in his difference between "matter of polity" and matter of law.[6]

In the early seventeenth century it was usual to speak of this "public," "extraordinary," "regal," "indisputable" prerogative as consisting of "reasons of state," and several things seem evident in regard to it. First, it was nothing more nor less than the old familiar *gubernaculum* of Bracton; secondly, it seems to have been accepted almost as generally under James I as it had been in the Tudor period; thirdly, from the point of view of mere legal precedent, it was strictly constitutional; fourthly, men were becoming gradually but increasingly conscious of the deadly threat to their inherited liberties that it involved. Time will not serve to give more than a few of the many illustrations of these facts. For others I can only refer to almost any page of the state trials dealing with the great constitutional issues of the age—such as Bate's Case in 1606,[7] the Case of the Post-Nati in 1608,[8] the Five Knights' Case in 1627,[9] and the Ship-Money Case in 1637 [10]—or to their repercussions in parliament, as disclosed in the debates reported in the *Parliamentary History.* Thus Bacon said in 1606: "The King's acts that grieve the subject are either against law, and so void; or according to strictness of law, and yet grievous." [11]

In 1627 Sir Robert Heath, the attorney general, declared:

The King cannot command your lordship, or any other court of justice, to proceed otherwise than according to the laws of this

Kingdom. . . . But, my lord, there is a great difference between those legal commands, and that *absoluta potestas* that a sovereign hath, by which a king commands.[12]

We are too wise, nay we are too foolish, in understanding to examine matters of state, to which we are not born. . . . Shall any say, The King cannot do this? No, we may only say, He will not do this.[13]

It is a dangerous thing for men in matters of weight to avouch precedents with confidence, when they make nothing for them.[14]

The truth is that legal precedents in matters of government were in the King's favor and justified the attorney general's interpretation of the constitution, "according to strictness of law; and yet grievous," as Bacon had said. There was no remedy in existing law, but there were serious grievances crying to be remedied.

As Sir Benjamin Rudyard later said in Parliament, "This by the way I will say of Reason of State, that, in the latitude by which it is used, it hath eaten out almost, not only the laws, but all the religion of Christendom." [15] "This is the crisis of parliaments; we shall know by this if parliaments live or die." [16] "King's Prerogatives, are rather beside the law, than against it." [17] As another member put it, to admit reason of state in a particular case would "open a gap, through which Magna Charta, and the rest of the statutes, may issue out and vanish." [18] Or, as yet another declared, "By this we shall acknowledge a regal, as well as a legal power: Let us give that to the King, that the law gives him, and no more." [19] "I understand not matters of state," Selden said.[20] "Our laws are not acquainted with sovereign power," said Sir Thomas Wentworth.[21] And Sir Edward Coke said: "I know that prerogative is part of the law, but 'sovereign power' is no parliamentary word. . . . Magna Charta is such a fellow, that he will have no sovereign." [22] "If this be law, what do we talk of our Liberties?" asked Sir Robert Phillips. "Why do we trouble ourselves with the dispute of Law, Franchises, Propriety of Goods?" [23]

It was strictly true, as Wentworth said, that English law was "not acquainted with sovereign power"; yet it was also true that the English constitution included such a sovereign power. The arguments of the friends and those of the opponents of a *potestas absoluta* never met; they slid past each other. The opponents were certainly arguing against precedent when they denied the existence of such a power, but their instinct was not at fault when they felt that "at this little gap every man's liberty may in time go out." [24] The very strictness of law was grievous, as Bacon had said. Here was a case that no legal judgment could remedy, for the law itself imposed no adequate check if the attorney general was right in his statement that none could say the King *cannot* do this; if he could only say the King *will* not do this.

The two conflicting points of view are well illustrated in two short statements: one by the chief justice in Darnell's Case, the other by William Hakewill. Addressing counsel for one of the prisoners, the chief justice said, "The precedents are all against you every one of them, and what shall guide our judgments, since there is nothing alleged in this case but precedents?" [25] But on the conclusions drawn from these precedents, as Hakewill said with equal truth, "I shall have an estate of inheritance for life, or for years in my land, or propriety in my goods, and I shall be a tenant at will for my liberty; I shall have propriety in my house, and not liberty in my person." [26] From such an *impasse* the only outcome and the only remedy was some measure of revolution.

127

It seems clear that the court could do nothing but decide on the specific precedents cited, and the later accusations of bias and corruption made indiscriminately against all the judges who held that view reflect more on the fairness of some modern historians than on the integrity of some of the justices of Charles I.[27]

On the other hand, no historian can deny the truth of Hakewill's counterstatement. Whether right or wrong, the judgment of the courts had to be reversed by the nation, if not by the courts, or English liberty would have been lost entirely and possibly forever. In all these great constitutional cases the defenders of prerogative relied on good specific precedents, while their opponents were driven to argue from the true general principles of the ancient constitution; and both may well have acted in entire good faith. One side relied on the letter, the other on the spirit, of English monarchical institutions; and in the courts the letter naturally prevailed. But their arguments never met each other. There never was a genuine joinder of issue.

Half a century ago Mr. Hubert Hall declared that "for sixty years the gross errors and injustice of the accepted history of the Case of Impositions have passed without a single challenge." [28] It is true that the general condemnation of the judges, not only in Bate's Case, but in every other great trial of the time involving the prerogative, has been undiscriminating, unfair, and pretty continuous. On the other hand, it seems an equal injustice to condemn men like Selden and Coke, who in the last analysis put liberty above law, even at the risk of seeming to be revolutionists.

The constitutional struggle of the seventeenth century was not as simple as the histories would sometimes make it. It was no clear-cut issue between despotism and freedom. Sir Robert

Heath, because he upheld the King's impositions, was no mere
absolutist; nor were his opponents antimonarchists or enemies
of settled and orderly government.[29] The key to this difficulty
remains the old distinction between *jurisdictio* and *gubernaculum* that we have met with before, and it is a key that has
been too sparingly used. The fact is that England was almost
ripe for revolution, but no one dared as yet to avow it. Men on
the one side looked to the ancient legal rights endangered by
a king who could invade them with impunity; men on the
other resisted every tendency to impose on a king checks which
had never been imposed before. The first were relying exclusively on the precedents of the ancient *jurisdictio;* the second
with equal justice could cite innumerable instances of royal
acts of government beyond or even against the common law.

The statement that I quoted earlier from Sir Walter Raleigh
was more prophetic than he knew:

If the House press the King to grant unto them all that is theirs
by the Law, they cannot, in Justice, refuse the King all that is his
by the Law. And where will be the Issue of such a Contention? I
dare not divine, but sure I am, that it will tend to a Prejudice both
of the King and Subject.

This was a deadlock of two constitutional views that had at
length become irreconcilable. Economic, social, and intellectual developments had made inevitable a struggle between
these two elements of the traditional constitution. The Stuart
kings did not bring it about; but, to the discredit of those kings
without a single exception, it must be said that the struggle
was hastened and its bloody accompaniment augmented by a
royal stupidity, arrogance, shiftiness, and stubbornness that
have few parallels in history. Hallam's judgment, however,
though in some ways warranted, seems less than fair, when he

129

says generally that "The courts of justice . . . did not consist of men conscientiously impartial between the king and the subject; some corrupt with hope of promotion, many more fearful of removal, or awe-struck by the frowns of power." [30] And it seems less than discriminating when he says in particular that Heath's argument in Bate's Case trampled upon "all statute and precedent." [31] It is unfortunately this kind of one-sided interpretation, both parliamentary and royalist, that has marked much of the treatment of this fascinating and critical phase in the development of our constitutional ideas and institutions. In it all there is no period more important than that of the early Stuart kings of England, and none more in need of a discriminating reconstruction—and a reconstruction, I may add, which will take proper account of earlier precedent as well as contemporary conditions. In that precedent I believe the persistence of our old familiar *jurisdictio* and *gubernaculum* will be found to be of paramount importance.

In what has just been said the subject logically next in order of treatment has already been roughly indicated—the reversal, by the representatives of the people of England in parliament, of the constitutional doctrines contained in the judgments of the English courts, the reinforcement of the subject's rights by the addition for the first time of a legal and a political control over government sufficient to protect these rights from royal encroachment. If, as I have maintained, the previous judgments of the courts were sound, the imposition of this new and unprecedented control over the ancient *potestas absoluta* involved nothing less than a revolution in English political institutions and ideas.

When Sir Edward Coke in the parliament of 1621 said, "We are here for thousands and ten thousands," he was unwittingly uttering a threat to the existing English constitution. It is unnecessary here to recount the dramatic events between 1621 and 1689 by which the threat became an actuality; they are in every English history. It is perhaps more important to consider the exact nature of the constitutional changes that these events brought about. The chief of these changes was the ultimate making of the king responsible in government as well as in jurisdiction, and responsible not merely to God, as had been held before, but to the law and to the people. The king remained *legibus solutus* as before, but this was now narrowly construed to mean merely that the royal person was outside the coercive force of law. It no longer meant, as it had meant in the Tudor period, that his official acts were beyond the legal scrutiny of the courts or removed from the political control of the people's representatives in parliament. On its strictly legal side this great change is probably best to be seen in the new meaning of the old maxim, "The King can do no wrong."

Let us recall how Stephen Gardiner had justified his official conduct to the Protector Somerset in 1547. He said then that a royal order to a minister enjoining an act of government in violation of a statute was but a doubtful protection for that minister in case of a later prosecution, and he cited the case of his old master, Cardinal Wolsey. What he said was true enough, but it was never true in the Tudor period unless the king withdrew his protection from his minister. The king could and did prevent actions brought against his ministers whenever he pleased, and Henry VIII's desertion of Wolsey when that minister was accused of a breach of the Statute of Praemunire committed at the king's own command is one of the most despicable of the many despicable acts of that tyrant.

By 1689 this was all changed, or was rapidly changing. The reaction after the execution of Charles I had proved the necessity of exempting the king personally from criminal responsibility. In that sense the king could still "do no wrong," he was *legibus solutus*. But the old maxim had gradually acquired an additional meaning: not so much that the king could not break the law as that no breach of the law could be considered an act of the king. A particular royal wrong was not legal, because no wrong could be regal; the absolute "perfection" of the king must be assumed. Or, as Andrew Amos puts it, "No mismanagement in government is imputable personally to the Sovereign, whilst, nevertheless, no wrong can be done to the people without a remedy. Whence it follows, as a corollary, that all acts of State must be performed by responsible Ministers." [32] As Amos shows, the reign of Charles II was an important period in this new development, though the later principle was not as yet firmly and finally fixed.

This fact makes all the more interesting some constitutional statements of Sir Matthew Hale, remarkable for the time, which have received less attention than their importance deserves. In two essays, *Reflections on Mr. Hobbs His Dialogue of the Lawe* [33] and *De Prerogativa Regis*,[34] the author makes a classification of authority which, so far as my knowledge goes, is original with him. Since the middle ages the power of government had been distinguished as a *potestas coerciva* and a *potestas directiva*. Hale adopts these two, but adds a third, which, so far as I know, was entirely new—a *potestas irritans actus contrarios,* a power of rendering null and void acts contrary to law. "And therefore," he says,

though the King, in case of such acts done contrary to the directive power of the law, is not subject to the coercive power of the law in respect of the sacredness and sublimity of his person, the instruments and ministers that are the immediate actors of such unlawful things are subject to the coercive power of the law, for the Kings act in such cases being void doth not justify or defend the instruments. This is one of the principal reasons of the maxim in law, that the King can do no wrong, for if it be wrong and contrary to the law, it is not the act of the King but of the minister or instrument that puts it in execution and consequently such minister is liable to the coercion of the law and to make satisfaction.[35]

If my reading of the Tudor constitution is accurate, no such statement as this would have been true to fact in 1603 or before, and possibly not even as late as 1643. This is a new responsibility of the king for government, and not for mere *jurisdictio*. It really extends the old *jurisdictio* over the whole field of the *gubernaculum*. This marks a true revolution. But it was not enough. The new responsibility is only a responsibility to the law, enforceable legally by the courts against the ministers of the crown. The effectiveness of this as a practical sanction for individual right was therefore doubtful until the tenure of judges was made independent of the king by the Act of Settlement in 1701. And even this was ultimately not enough. The process of reinforcement and guarantee of individual right against governmental will was not complete until to this negative legal *potestas irritans* there was added a positive political control of government exercisable by the representatives of the people in parliament; until legal responsibility was supplemented by political responsibility; until the people could dismiss a minister merely because they disapproved of his policies, without waiting for an actual breach of law or inventing one, as they did in Strafford's case. To recount in detail the growth of the last of these new political principles, the model for almost all modern European constitutional developments before 1914, would be to retell practically the whole constitutional history of England since the Revolution of 1689. In the space allotted to this subject, I can do no more than give a few instances to illustrate some early stages in the emergence of this modern popular political control of government out of the powers formerly conceded to the king alone.

As we have seen, the English king was in fact the "supreme governor" long before he obtained the official title, and this involved unchecked exercise of a power always claimed by English sovereigns before 1640 and rarely denied even by English subjects before 1603—a power "innate in the person of an absolute King, and in the persons of the Kings of England," as Sir John Banks said in the Case of Ship Money,[36] "the majestical right, and power of a free monarch."[37] The concrete powers of the king included under this "majestical right" were thus enumerated by Justice Crawley in 1637: "to give laws to his subjects," to make peace and war, to create supreme magistrates, "that the last appeal be to the King," to pardon offences, to coin money, "to have allegiance, fealty, and homage," and "to impose taxes without common consent in parliament."[38] The list given after the Restoration by Sir Matthew Hale is substantially the same with the very significant omission of the right to impose taxes without consent of parliament, and the addition of "the power of the Militia of this Kingdome," which had been the immediate issue in the first civil war.[39] Before the judgment in the case of Darcy v. Allen in 1603 [40] concerning patents of monopoly, these also, along with all other kinds of royal patent, would no doubt have been comprised in any enumeration of the specific powers of the "absolute king."

Some of these powers were conceded to the king even by the most extreme of his opponents. The power to tax they never admitted, of course, and rightly; the power over the militia they never questioned until 1642; patents of monopoly they had resisted since Elizabeth's reign, but the first statutory action against such patents was in 1624. No limitations of royal control over judicature were imposed by law till after the Revolution. Political control of foreign relations might be said to have begun at the parliament of 1621, which was the first parliament to venture even to discuss this subject; but legal limitation was never attempted. In the Ship-Money Case Sir George Vernon, one of the justices, declared that "a statute derogatory from the prerogative doth not bind the King." [41] Yet, more than a dozen years before, the Statute of Monopolies had certainly derogated from the prerogative, and in a startling way, not only by declaring actual or future monopolies with some exceptions to be void, but by expressly including proclamations or inhibitions connected with them, and by providing that all disputed matters concerning monopolies must be examined "according to the common laws of this realm, and not otherwise." [42] This, so far as I know, is the first statutory invasion of the royal prerogative. Not many others followed it, because with the Revolution of 1689 the king himself came to owe his title to parliament, and parliament's complete political control of administration made further legal limitation of it unnecessary.

From this long and necessarily hurried survey I do not feel qualified to deduce any strict definition of constitutionalism, but perhaps I may be warranted in making a few general observations of a more modest character. The opening words of Bodin's book *On the Republic* have always seemed to me in many ways the most significant thing in that great work. He defines a republic as "a government"—a very different thing from what Aristotle meant when he used practically the same words. Some will differ from my opinion as to what he means when he says this must be "un *droit* gouvernement," and as to whether the limitations contained in that word *droit* can be considered permissible in any logical theory of sovereignty. But I think everyone must be impressed by any definition made in 1576 which completely identifies the state with the government. That identification is a formulation, in terms of a general theory, of the political conditions which had actually come to prevail in almost every unitary state of Europe. Everywhere the emphasis was placed on the need of strong and efficient national rule. The memory of the recent power and excesses of a multitude of "overgrown lords," and the threat of disintegration occasioned by radical differences in religion, led both to an acquiescence in such a concentration of political power in the government as the middle ages had never known and to an emphasis upon that government's rights, rather than its duties, which would, I think, have been considered excessive a century or two earlier.

Constitutional history is usually the record of a series of oscillations. At one time private right is the chief concern of the citizens; at another the prevention of disorder that threatens to become anarchy. In general, the sixteenth century is marked by the latter of these two characteristics. In England, at least, the seventeenth marks a swing toward the opposite extreme, and the eighteenth, apparently, a swing backward toward a *potestas absoluta,* but now, as never before, a power vested in the national assembly instead of the king. These changes may be marked in the mutual relations of *jurisdictio* and *gubernaculum.* When the rights of government are unduly stressed, the rights of individuals are often threatened; when the latter are overemphasized, government becomes too weak to keep order. A citizen has been defined as "a bearer of rights and duties"; a government might well be described in much the same terms. In the middle ages, when that government was always in the hands of a monarch, the duties were probably best indicated by the terms of the old coronation oath. The secular part of that oath enjoined upon the king the two duties of maintaining justice and keeping order, and a later provision added the upholding of "the laws which the mass of the people have chosen." I think, therefore, that I was justified in saying earlier that men like Selden and Hakewill, and their fellows of the parliamentary party, by opposing the pretensions of the Stuarts, were appealing to the true spirit of the constitution even though the letter was against them.

The constitution was held to be a thing of balanced power and right, and the modern theory of sovereignty is the result of a belated recognition of the truth that in fact the perfect balance can never be long maintained. Wentworth in 1628 spoke of the "sweet harmony" of the constitution which he then thought the king was imperiling. In 1641 as earl of Strafford he reasserted on his trial his fear of any threat to this balance, but he now believed that the great enemy was not the king but the parliament. The power that now seemed to him to threaten the ancient balanced constitution was the menace of the illegal pretensions of the two houses against the crown. Though he had changed sides, he had not given up his belief in the "sweet harmony" of the ancient English frame of government. Hobbes, on the contrary, already saw that these men who dreamt of a balance of power in the state were pursuing an ideal, possible perhaps as a doctrine of abstract law, but never practicable for long as a matter of actual politics; and it was always with actual politics, and not with law, that Hobbes was concerned. The English struggle, as he was one of the first clearly to see, could never be ended except by the complete supremacy of one or the other of the contending parties. All this he later put in striking form, in his *Behemoth*, or history of the civil wars.

As a result of the English Revolution and the Revolution settlement, the representative parliament finally assumed, and for the first time, both the duties and many of the rights of the English king, and there remained as before the question of the proper relation of these to each other. It is true that no practical limits can ever be put to the political power of the people, not even those that in the end had proved insufficient to curb the king. As Sir Roger Twysden said in the seventeenth century, "The world, now above 5,500 years old, hath found means to limit kings, but never yet any republique." [43] And yet the people may restrain themselves. In their case, no less than in that of the monarch, it is "a worthy voice of reigning majesty to profess to rule according to law." Sometimes they have restrained themselves, sometimes not; and in their rule we may observe somewhat the same oscillations as marked that of the kings in an earlier period. During much of the nineteenth century there was a tendency to narrow the sphere of government and overemphasize the rights of the citizen. The duties of the ruling organ were forgotten in the desire to protect the individual in some at least of his rights. This often led to a callous disregard of those who had few inherited rights to be protected. The policy of *laissez faire* became little more than a maintenance of the *status quo,* and that meant the retention of traditional abuses as well as traditional rights. In fact, many of those individual rights had become nothing less than crying abuses.

Then the pendulum swung in the opposite direction. Professor Dicey, in his brilliant lectures on *Law and Opinion in England,* has traced the development toward collectivism which resulted. The state veered toward regimentation instead of the policy of hands-off. Huxley has described the process in a remarkable paper. The utilitarian individualists receded into the background; Herbert Spencer and his *Man Versus the State* were discarded. Here in the United States we have passed through all these phases, which, under modern conditions, change sometimes with great rapidity; and there are some indications that at this moment we may be passing out of a phase of regimentation into a returning period of *laissez faire,* and that the reaction may be extreme.

This is bringing up and will in future bring up fundamental political questions that we shall all have to meet. The earlier history of the growth of our constitutionalism can, of course, furnish no definite or conclusive answer to many of these questions, because the conditions under which they exist now are in so many ways different from those which surrounded their growth in past ages. Nevertheless, I do believe that careful unbiased study of this past growth is not without its practical value in helping us to analyze our own pressing problems, if not to answer them.

I may seem to strain a point if I say that in my opinion our ancient distinction between *jurisdictio* and *gubernaculum* may still be a valuable help in making this analysis of our present-day problems. I venture to say, however, that we have with us still the *jurisdictio* and the "government," and that the reconciliation of the two remains probably our most serious practical problem, just as it was in seventeenth-century England. I would go further, and add that there is the same necessity now, as in past ages, to preserve these two sides of political institutions intact, to maintain every institution instrumental in strengthening them both, and to guard against the overwhelming of one of them by the other.

There is a constant threat to all the rights of personality we hold dearest—such rights as freedom of thought and expression and immunity for accused persons, from arbitrary detention and from cruel and abusive treatment. These have always been endangered when "reasons of state" have been thought to require it. At times it seems to me that just now we are in special danger of forgetting these rights and these dangers. In some parts of the world apparently all such safeguards of individual right and personality have been thrown down entirely and no one is safe from prosecution *ex officio mero,* secret, arbitrary, and irresponsible. "Reasons of state" have been urged in the past for just such enormities, but probably never on such a scale as at this moment. Never in recorded history, I believe, has the individual been in greater danger from government than now, never has *jurisdictio* been in greater jeopardy from *gubernaculum,* and never has there been such need that we should clearly see this danger and guard against it. The beneficial results of the revolution which I have been trying to trace in the history of our own constitutionalism are as yet more apparent here than in some less fortunate parts of the world, but they cannot be maintained and preserved even here if we are not constantly on our guard. And surely an appreciation of what these things have meant in the past ought to give us a clearer apprehension of what they should mean now, and a knowledge of the kinds of danger that have threatened these rights in former times should be of some use in showing us where to look for present enemies of our welfare and how to oppose them when found.

If *jurisdictio* is essential to liberty, and *jurisdictio* is a thing of the law, it is the law that must be maintained against arbitrary will. And the one institution above all others essential to the preservation of the law has always been and still is an honest, able, learned, independent judiciary. The sad history of the Stuart attempts to corrupt and to intimidate their courts of law ought to be a lesson to all professed lovers of liberty who

140

think we can get our needed social reforms and keep them safe without the assistance of courts free from governmental control. In this I hope I shall not be misunderstood. I am not defending indefensible decisions of our courts; I would not shield them from the severest criticism. Nor am I denying the need for much reform in the judicial process; it is far too slow and cumbersome. But the past history of these institutions does seem to show that, whether through ignorance or intention, some of the recent proposals and measures for the professed purpose of remedying these ills seem better designed to weaken these safeguards to liberty than to improve them. If it is through ignorance, then the history of the earlier relations between *jurisdictio* and government may be of some practical value.

But to insist thus on the indispensability of legal limits to governmental power and the safeguarding of these limits by an independent court is not to advocate the enfeebling of that government itself. Among all the modern fallacies that have obscured the true teachings of constitutional history, few are worse than the extreme doctrine of the separation of powers and the indiscriminate use of the phrase "checks and balances." The doctrine of the separation of powers has no true application to judicial matters. Consideration of this important question should not be clouded and confused by including the independence of the judges, with which it has nothing to do. But the present confusion does not end with that. There is an equal lack of discrimination between the legal checks for which our history gives such strong support, and the political balances for which, so far as I can see, there is little historical background whatever, except the fancies of eighteenth-century doctrinaires and their followers. Political balances have no institutional background whatever except in the imaginations

141

of closet philosophers like Montesquieu. When in modern times representative assemblies took over the rights and duties of earlier kings, they assumed a power and a responsibility that had always been concentrated and undivided. There is no medieval doctrine of the separation of powers, though there is a very definite doctrine of limitation of powers.

Some modern conservatives can see no practical difference between limitation and separation today, and I must confess that many historians have not seen any difference between them in earlier times. The gist of nearly all that has been said here thus far is to show that such difference has existed from the middle ages to the present. I am now concerned with showing that it ought still to be maintained. The limiting of government is not the weakening of it. The maxim that the king can do no wrong is a legal, not a political, maxim. The true safeguards of liberty against arbitrary government are the ancient legal limitation and the modern political responsibility. But this responsibility, which in modern times has become fully as important for our welfare as the ancient legal limits, is, I think, utterly incompatible with any extended system of checks and balances.

In Rome, where checks and balances might be said to have had their origin, they marked the antagonism of class against class. The plebeian tribune could block any action of the patrician consul. The expedient itself is just about as healthful a procedure in a modern state as the class division out of which it originally arose and through which it persists. What we need, in addition to the negative legal limitation of the sphere of government already mentioned, is the full political responsibility to the people and to the *whole* people for all positive acts of government within its proper sphere. But without adequate power there can be no such responsibility, and if the

142

power is not concentrated and obvious to all, there can be neither the fixing nor the enforcement of this responsibility. The one thing in our political machinery which, more than any other, has fostered the growth of "pressure groups," with all their attendant corruption, is the inability to fix responsibility. This has led to "log-rolling" and every other form of crooked politics; for under any system of balances run wild the result is sure to be government for private interests or groups instead of government for the whole people. Our government has become to an alarming extent a mere process of "passing the buck," and that means shifting the responsibility for acts which could not be defended for one moment if responsibility for them could ever be fixed.

For this dissipation of governmental power with its consequent irresponsibility I can find no good precedents in the constitutional history of the past. The system has worked disaster ever since it was adopted, and it is not the outcome of earlier political experience. Unlike the legal limitations in our bills of rights, it is not the matured result of centuries of trial and error. It is a figment of the imagination of eighteenth-century doctrinaires who found it in our earlier history only because they were ignorant of the true nature of that history. These political balances were unknown before the eighteenth century, were almost untried before the nineteenth, and have been disastrous wherever they have been tried since. Unlike our legal safeguards, they formed no part of our constitutional inheritance from the past, and my fear is that, if they develop much further, a reaction will surely set in as it has in Europe; and this, once started, may sweep before it every protection of any sort, legal as well as political, to leave the individual naked and unprotected against the ever-present danger of arbitrary government.

In parts of Europe, it will be noted, the incompetence of constitutional governments led to their replacement by despotisms. In Italy, if the weakness and corruption of parliamentary institutions had not first made them contemptible, Fascism would hardly have taken their place. Feebleness is no guarantee of constitutionalism; it has usually been the chief cause of its overthrow. Reactionaries have always proved to be the deadliest of all the enemies of a true conservatism. The proper remedy for the abuse of "reasons of state" has never consisted and does not now consist in making the government incompetent. Our past constitutional history seems to show that it consists of a *jurisdictio* under the protection of an independent court, coupled with a *gubernaculum* strong enough to perform all its essential duties and obvious enough to ensure full responsibility to all the people for the faithfulness of that performance.

The practical inferences I have ventured to draw from our constitutional history may to many seem too conservative, but I hope they will not seem reactionary. If reaction is really to be avoided, we must preserve our legal guarantees. We must keep them intact, but we dare not stop there. There is corruption which feebleness in government makes possible, and this can only be ended by making government, within its legal limits, actually stronger than it is. This strength, however, is itself a danger if it is not completely responsible to the people, and to all the people, and at all times.

If the history of our constitutional past teaches anything, it seems to indicate that the mutual suspicions of reformers and constitutionalists, of which I see dangerous symptoms in the United States today, must be ended if we are to keep and enlarge the liberties for which our ancestors fought. Liberals must become more constitutional than some of them are, con-

stitutionalists must become more liberal than most of them
have been. We cannot get the needed redress of injustices and
abuses without reform, and we can never make these reforms
lasting and effective unless we reduce them to the orderly
processes of law. Let us not confuse *jurisdictio* and *gubernaculum,* and let us not allow either to swallow up the other.

I am not so rash as to try to apply the general principles
guiding our past constitutional history to the details of our
present constitutional arrangements in the United States; for
that I am not competent. But I do believe that these general
principles, if they are properly deducible thus from the past
experience of our race, ought to have their due weight in determining our attitude toward our present specific problems.
We live under a written constitution which classifies some
things under *jurisdictio,* as legal fundamentals, and thus puts
them under the protection of the courts, while it leaves other
matters to the free discretion of the organs of positive government it has created. The distribution of these matters between
jurisdictio and *gubernaculum,* made so many years ago, is of
course in constant need of revision by interpretation or by
amendment; and it may also be that the mode of that amendment is somewhat too slow and cumbersome for the best interests of all. But the surest safeguard of a proper balance between the *jurisdictio* and the *gubernaculum*—and that even in
a government *of* the people as well as *for* them—would seem
to consist in some such constitution containing some such distribution. There is the problem of restriction and the problem
of responsibility, and practical politics involves their interrelation. One of them is legal, and it is far the older; the other
is political and in its present form it is much more recent. The
people have now replaced the king in these political matters
of government; but even in a popular state, such as we trust

ours is, the problem of law *versus* will remains the most important of all practical problems. We must leave open the possibility of an appeal from the people drunk to the people sober, if individual and minority rights are to be protected in the periods of excitement and hysteria from which we unfortunately are not immune. The long and fascinating story of the balancing of *jurisdictio* and *gubernaculum*, of which I could give only the barest outline here, should be, if we could study it with an open mind, of some help in adjusting and maintaining today the delicate balance of will and law, the central practical problem of politics now as it has been in all past ages. The two fundamental correlative elements of constitutionalism for which all lovers of liberty must yet fight are the legal limits to arbitrary power and a complete political responsibility of government to the governed.

Notes

1. Quoted in the Oxford Dictionary *s.v.* "constitution."

2. *Rights of Man* in *The Complete Works of Thomas Paine* (London), pp. 302–303, 370.

3. *An Appeal from the New to the Old Whigs* (1791), in *The Works of the Right Honourable Edmund Burke* (1855), III, 81.

4. *Ibid.*, p. 13.

5. *A Dissertation upon Parties* (1733–1734), in *The Works of Lord Bolingbroke* (1841), II, 88.

6. *Ibid.*, p. 105. The Septennial Act was defended by its supporters as the exercise of an extraordinary rather than an ordinary power of parliament. The Jacobite rising in 1715, it was held, had created a national emergency in which the very safety of the state depended upon the postponement of a parliamentary election. As the judges of Charles I had justified the royal prerogative in the levy of ship money, so the Whigs now justified an extension of parliament's power by misquotation of Cicero's *Salus populi suprema lex esto,* turning his *esto* into an *est,* and perverting the mere exhortation addressed to the commander of an army in the field into a general maxim of arbitrary government. The argument for emergency powers is not an unsound one—far from it; but it becomes a grave menace to individual liberty when "the sole judge, both of the danger, and when and how the same is to be prevented, and avoided," is a king; and may be such even when the sole judge is a representative assembly; the more so if only a partisan, a corrupt, or an "unreformed" one. John Selden noticed this substitution of *est* for the *esto* of Cicero's maxim and deplored its misuse in his day to justify absolutism under pretext of national emergency. He mistook it, however, for an extract from the XII Tables. "There is not any thing in the World more abus'd then this Sentence *Salus populi suprema lex esto,* for wee apply it, as if wee ought to forsake the knowne law when it may bee most for the advantage of the people, when it meanes no such thing: for first, tis not *salus populi lex est,* but *esto* . . ." (*Table Talk, s.v.* "People," folio 56b). Selden's strictures would probably have been even more severe if he had known that the maxim was applied originally by Cicero to a military commander alone, and then only when he was actually in the field: *militiae,* but never *domi* (Cicero, *De Legibus, lib.* III, cap. 3, sec. 8).

Others besides Selden in his time made the same mistake of attributing this important maxim to the XII Tables instead of to Cicero. See, for example, Richard Zouche's *Elementa Jurisprudentiae* (Oxford, 1636), part IV, p. 55; William Fulbecke, *A Direction or Preparative to the Study of the Laws* (London, 1620), folio 2; Bacon, *Essays, Of Judicature.* Bacon, as many others, omits the verb altogether, but evidently implies an *est,* not an *esto.* Serjeant Maynard, a century after Bacon, has *esto* instead of *est,* but still thinks it comes from the XII Tables (*Parliamentary History,* vol. V, col. 125).

Arbitrary government, possible under the Tudors as an ordinary power, became impossible under the Stuarts except as an extraordinary power warranted only by the doctrine of emergencies. This was one of the most momentous of the results of "the winning of the initiative" by the House of Commons, but in the later use of the phrase it was in process of becoming a justification of arbitrary government by a parliament as it had formerly justified royal absolutism.

The Septennial Act of 1716 is no doubt the first important application of the theory of parliamentary omnipotence after the Revolution, but within a dozen years of that event there are indications that the House of Commons is already beginning to think of itself not merely as the "full and free Representative of this nation," which the Declaration of Rights in 1689 had declared it to be, but as a body with an inherent authority independent of the people who had chosen it. This appears as early as 1701 in the imprisonment by the House of the Kentish petitioners. That such a view was not shared by all, however, is indicated in many contemporary tracts, especially the remarkable "Legion's Memorial," so-called, probably written by Defoe (*Parliamentary History,* V, 1252; *Later Stuart Tracts,* ed. by George A. Aitken, pp. 179–186), which closes with the significant warning, "Englishmen are no more to be Slaves to Parliaments, than to Kings." As the rhyming pamphleteer of the same year said,

> Posterity will be ashamed to own,
> The actions we their ancestors have done,
> When they for ancient precedents enquire,
> And to the Journals of this age retire,
> To see one tyrant banish'd from his home,
> To set five hundred traitors in his room.

The History of the Kentish Petition (Somers Tracts, XI, 254; *Parliamentary History,* vol. V, app. xvii, col. 188; *Later Stuart Tracts,* p. 178) probably also by Defoe.

The fundamental cleavage between such views as these and the new temper of the House of Commons appears clearly in the answer to these "Legion" pamphlets made by Sir Humphrey Mackworth (*Somers Tracts,* XI, 176 ff.) in which he declared "that the King, lords, and commons, united together, have an absolute supreme power to do whatever they shall think necessary or convenient for the public good of which they are the only judges, there being no legal power on earth to controul them. . . . The king, lords, and commons, therefore, as supreme, have superior powers, and the liberty of exercising them (according to the nature and constitution thereof) as they in their respective wisdoms and discretion shall think most conducing to the public good, without rendering any account for the same" (pp. 282–283). To this

Defoe replied: "The people of England have delegated all the executive power in the King, the legislative in the King, Lords, and Commons, the sovereign judicative in the Lords, the remainder is reserved in themselves, and not committed, no not to their representatives: all powers delegated are to one great end and purpose, and no other, and that is the public good. If either or all the branches to whom this power is delegated invert the design, the end of their power, the right they have to that power ceases, and they become tyrants and usurpers of a power they have no right to" (*The Original Power of the Collective Body of the People of England Examined and Asserted* [London, 1701], in *The Works of Daniel DeFoe,* by William Hazlitt [London, 1843], III, 9). It is the English form of the old controversy of the early glossators, whether the *populus* had conferred on the Emperor all its *imperium* and *potestas* unconditionally and irrevocably or not. For references to some further contemporary statements, see *The Theory of Balanced Government,* by Stanley Pargellis, *The Constitution Reconsidered* (New York, 1938), pp. 37–49.

The same conflicting views are brought out again in 1704–1705 in the great case of Ashby v. White (Howell's *State Trials,* XIV, col. 697 ff.) in which the Lords declared, "It could not then [in 1628, when the Petition of Right was framed by the Commons] have been imagined, that the successors of those men would ever have pretended to an arbitrary and unlimited power of depriving their fellow subjects of their liberties" (col. 869). And they add, "This is the first time a House of Commons have made use of their having given the People's money, as an argument why the prince should deny Writs of Right to the subject, obstruct the course of justice, and deprive them of their birth-rights" (col. 871).

Thus, as Bolingbroke said in 1733, the new conception of parliament's power, "in less than twenty years," "is grown or is growing familiar to us." From this it was but a step to the denial, in the reign of George III, of the right of the electors of Middlesex to choose their own representatives; to that statement of the Lord Chancellor in 1766 that "every government can arbitrarily impose laws on all its subjects"; and to the assertion made about the same time in the Commons that that body alone in the enacting of law "constitutes the only people of England which the law acknowledges." In these things Burke had ample warrant for his declaration in 1770, in his *Thoughts on the Cause of the Present Discontents,* that "the Distempers of monarchy were the great subjects of apprehension and redress, in the last century; in this, the distempers of parliament." "This change from an immediate state of procuration and delegation to a course of acting as from original power, is the way in which all the popular magistracies in the world have been perverted from their purposes." "To be a Whig on the business of an hundred years ago, is very consistent with every advantage of present servility." For all the rest of the people of England, outside the Commons, there seemed no remedy left for such "distempers" and their deprivation of these ancient "birth-rights" except the resort to force; for from the fact that there was no appeal from their jurisdiction in controverted elections, the Commons were implying, as Burke says, that they were bound by no rule but their own discretion. That ultimate remedy of force the authors of the "Legion's Memorial" had threatened to use as early as 1701; its actual use came first in 1775 by Englishmen in the colonies of North America; Englishmen were "no more to be slaves to Parliaments, than to Kings." In England itself the threat of such slavery finally became a thing of the past through the reforms of the nineteenth century, the gradual growth of truly "responsible" government, and the adoption in law and practice of the principle of Sir John Holt's dissenting opinion in the case of Ashby v. White.

7. *Parliamentary History*, XVI, 170. The italics are mine.

8. *An Appeal from the New to the Old Whigs, Works*, III, 30.

9. *A Collection of State Tracts* (London, 1705), I, 106.

10. *Some Remarks upon Government* (written in 1689), in *State Tracts*, I, 159, 160, 162.

11. *A Discourse Concerning the Nature, Power, and Proper Effects of the Present Conventions in Both Kingdoms* (1689), in *State Tracts*, I, 220.

12. *Some Political Writings of James Otis* (ed. by Charles F. Mullett; The University of Missouri Studies), p. 79.

13. Hezekiah Niles, *The Principles and Acts of the Revolution in America*, p. 19.

14. "What a word is that franchise? The lord may tax his villain high or low, but it is against the franchises of the land, for freemen to be taxed, but by their consent in parliament. Franchise is a French word, and in Latin it is Libertas" (1627; in *Parliamentary History*, II, 237).

15. *The Political Works of James I* (Cambridge, Mass., 1918), p. 300.

16. Howell's *State Trials*, II, 481, in which this speech is given as the speech of Yelverton. The notes of the debates in this parliament published by S. R. Gardiner show that the speech was made by Sir James Whitelocke (*Parliamentary Debates in 1610* [Camden Society, 1862], p. 103).

17. *Candid Quarterly Review*, no. 1 (February, 1914), p. 31.

18. *The Letters and Speeches of Oliver Cromwell* (ed. by S. C. Lomas), II, 382.

19. In such cases in the past it has been challenged occasionally though without success. For example, just after the Restoration, when the abolition of feudal tenures was agitated, one opponent of the measure declared: "And if an Act of the Commons alone, or of the Lords alone, or of both together, cannot amount to an Act of Parliament, the King himself cannot grant away his Regality, or Power, or means of governing by his Charter, or any Act which he can singly doe, his concurrence with both the Lords and Commons can no more make an Act to confirme that which should not be done or granted, than his own grant or Charter could have done, or than if he and the House of Commons only had made an Act." He then goes on to cite authorities for the principle "that the Superlative power of Parliaments above all but the

King, is in some things so restrained, as it cannot enact things against Right Reason, or common Right, or against the Lawes of God or Nature" (Fabian Philipps, Esq., *Tenenda non Tollenda* [London, 1660], pp. 254–255). On the various interpretations of Coke's statement of this principle in Bonham's Case, see C. H. McIlwain, *The High Court of Parliament* (1910), pp. 286 ff.; W. S. Holdsworth, "Courts of Law and Representative Assemblies in the Sixteenth Century," *Columbia Law Review,* XII (January, 1912), 1–31; T. F. T. Plucknett, "Bonham's Case and Judicial Review," *Harvard Law Review,* XL (1926), 30–70; S. E. Thorne, "Dr. Bonham's Case," *Law Quarterly Review,* October, 1938, pp. 543–552; S. E. Thorne, *A Discourse upon the Exposicion & Understandinge of Statutes* (San Marino, Calif., 1942), Introduction.

CHAPTER II (pages 23–40)

1. Hoveden, for example, usually refers to Henry II's Constitutions of Clarendon as *leges* (*Chronica Magistri Rogeri de Houedene* [Rolls Series], I, 220–222). Walter of Coventry calls them *consuetudines quae inductae sunt contra ecclesias terrae suae in tempore suo* (*The Historical Collection of Walter of Coventry* [Rolls Series], I, 207).

2. Liebermann, *Gesetze der Angelsachsen,* I, 553.

3. Lib. II, cap. vii (*Glanvill De Legibus et Consuetudinibus Angliae,* ed. by George E. Woodbine [New Haven, 1932], p. 63).

4. Lib. XIII, cap. xxxii, p. 172.

5. Folio 312 B.

6. Folio 168 B.

7. Philippe de Beaumanoir, *Coutumes de Beauvaisis,* ed. Am. Salmon (Paris, 1899–1900), § 958 (I, 486).

8. *De Republica Libri Sex et Viginti,* Authore D. Petro Gregorio Tholosano, lib. I, cap. i, §§ 16, 19 (Lugduni, 1609, pp. 4, 5).

9. Cicero, *De Re Publica,* I, 45 (69).

10. *Ibid.,* II, 21 (37). When, early in the fifteenth century, Jean de Terre Rouge wishes to express the idea conveyed by Cicero's *constitutio* or our "constitution," he uses, not that word, but the phrase *status publicus.* A century later Seyssell translates this by the term *La Police,* for which Sleidan in his admirable Latin translation of Seyssell employs *politia* and not *constitutio* as its equivalent. So Bodin, in speaking of the constitution of a republic, refers to it as *L'estat d'une Republique* (*Les six livres de la republique,* liv. II, chap. 11 [Paris, 1577, p. 200]). In his Latin version, it is *status Rei-publicae* (Paris, 1586, p. 189). It is true that Bernard de Girard Seigneur du Haillan, in the first edition of his important book, *De L'Estat et Succez des Affaires de France,* referring in the plural number to the limitations of government implied in Seyssell's term *La Police,* applies to them the word *constitutions,* but it seems clear that he is using the term *constitutions* to connote not the modern conception of the whole of the complex governmental framework in a

state as we do but its older sense, borrowed by the canonists from imperial Rome, by which he means only the several specific enactments of emperors or kings. If so this implies a reluctant acceptance on his part of the theory already asserted by Charles du Moulin and others that the existing limitations of monarchy contained in the customary law of France were originally effected by the enactments of former kings and not by the people *more utentium*. This is a far-reaching change from the medieval conception of Jean de Terre Rouge and Seyssell and the limitations of the English common law. It marks the longest theoretical step toward the absolutism which ultimately made the France of Louis XIV so different from England with its constitutionalism. Du Haillan's statement is in part as follows: ". . . qui sont les mesmes mots de Claude de Seissel en son livre de la Monarchie de France, lesquels (bien qu'ils sentent l'antiquité) nous n'avons voulu changer: toutesfois on voit bien que ce bel ordre institué en nostre Monarchie, est corrompu, & que nous ne retenons que l'ombre de ces belles premieres constitutions. Voila donc trois freins & brides, qui guident l'estat du royaume de France, & qui le gardent de se precipiter aux dangers, ausquels les estats, qui sont mal conduits & menez, se precipitent" (*De L'Estat et Succez des Affaires de France* [Paris, 1571], p. 82).

It is noteworthy here that du Haillan still uses the word *constitutions* in the plural and in its older medieval sense to include the several fundamental enactments of earlier kings. Thus far I have found no use of the word in its modern meaning, as the whole governmental framework of a state, before the seventeenth century. The first clear instance I have met with is Sir James Whitelocke's *jus publicum regni* referred to above at page 13. Even in 1649 the Court in its accusation of Charles I refers to "the fundamental constitutions of this Kingdom," not to the "Constitution" (Rushworth, *Historical Collections,* VII, 1396), and as late as the Revolution the pamphleteer quoted above at page 6 speaks of "the present Laws and Constitutions of England." The twelfth century *Constitutio Domus Regis* (*Red Book of the Exchequer* [Rolls Series], p. 807; *Black Book of the Exchequer,* ed. Thomas Hearne [London, 1774], I, 341) might be considered an exception, but to me that document as a whole looks more like an administrative order than a "constitution" in our modern sense of the term. The two extracts quoted by Du Cange in which the word is said to be equivalent to *consuetudo* also seem to me to refer to administrative provisions rather than promulgations of custom (*Glossarium Mediae et Infimae Latinitatis, s.v.* "constitutio"). They appear to be very like the *lex regia* of the *Leges Henrici Primi* (Liebermann, *Gesetze der Angelsachsen,* I, 556), or *aliquid de communi consilio . . . constitutum* in the Exchequer (*Dialogus de Scaccario,* I, i), or the *"novella constitutio," "hoc est a domino rege nostro,"* by virtue of which Thomas Brown, the king's almoner, sat in the Exchequer in the reign of Henry II, the predecessor of the later king's remembrancers or *Rememoratores Regis* (*Dialogus de Scaccario,* I, V, C). Apparently the word "constitution," although well-known in this earlier period, has a different meaning and cannot be normally interpreted in the sense of Cicero's "Constitution" or of our present one. In England the appearance of our modern conception of the "constitution" was delayed by the lawyers' habit of defining all public relations in terms of private law. As Professor Plucknett says, "When government has ceased to be regarded as private property . . . only then can we begin to speak of political thought and a constitution in the modern non-feudal sense" (*The Lancastrian Constitution, Tudor Studies*, p. 181).

11. *Outlines of Historical Jurisprudence*, vol. II. *The Jurisprudence of the Greek City*, p. 12.

12. *Ibid.*, p. 19.

13. *Ibid.*, pp. 41–42.

14. *Ibid.*, p. 136.

15. *The Politics of Aristotle*, I, 209–210.

16. *Laws*, VII, 817.

17. § 138. Almost the same words are used in *Areopagiticus*, § 14.

18. *Politics*, VI (iv), chap. xi.

19. Cicero, *De Re Publica*, III, 22.

20. Werner Jaeger, *Aristotle* (English translation), p. 290.

21. *Ibid.*, p. 13.

22. *Politicus*, p. 297. The italics are mine.

23. *Politics*, III, 16.

24. Page 715.

25. Page 659.

26. Hermann Rehm, *Geschichte der Staatsrechtswissenschaft*, p. 78.

27. *Ibid.*, p. 81.

28. *Ibid.*, pp. 95–96.

29. Λέγω δὲ νόμον τὸν μὲν ἴδιον τὸν δὲ κοινόν. "I refer, on the one hand to municipal law, on the other to the *jus gentium*" (*Rhetoric*, I, 13, 2).

30. *Politics*, VIII, 1307.

31. *The Politics of Aristotle*, tr. by J. E. C. Welldon, pp. 348–349.

32. *Ibid.*, p. 368.

33. *Ibid.*, pp. 392–393.

34. *Ibid.*, p. 393.

35. *Ibid.*, p. 394.

36. *Ibid.*, p. 396.

CHAPTER III (pages 41–66)

1. *A History of Medieval Political Theory in the West*, I, 8–9.

2. ". . . cum ipse imperator per legem imperium accipiat" (*Gai, Institutiones*, I, 2, 5).

3. *De Legibus*, III, 12. "It is the stoics who emancipated mankind from its subjection to despotic rule, and whose enlightened and elevated views of life

bridged the chasm that separated the ancient from the Christian state, and led the way to freedom" (Lord Acton, *The History of Freedom*, p. 24; see also pp. 28–29).

4. *Digest*, 1, 2, 2, 9.

5. Only one has survived to modern times, the one enacted at the accession of the Emperor Vespasian, A.D. 69–70. For the text of it see P. F. Girard, *Textes de droit romain*, 4th ed., pp. 107–108. The entrusting by the *populus* to the emperor of its authority to enact binding law is thus expressed by Ulpian in his *Institutiones* in the third century A.D.: "Quod principi placuit, legis habet vigorem; utpote cum lege regia, quae de imperio eius lata est, populus ei et in eum omne suum imperium et potestatem conferat" (*Dig.*, I, 4, 1.). In the sixth century this is paraphrased thus by the authors of the *Institutes* of Justinian: "Sed et quod principi placuit, legis habet vigorem, cum lege regia, quae de imperio eius lata est, populus ei et in eum omne suum imperium et potestatem concessit" (*Inst.*, I, 2, 6.). This substitution of *concedo* for *confero* in the sixth century statement of the principle, and above all the deliberate change to a past tense instead of the present as used by both Gaius and Ulpian—these seem to warrant the view that no predecessor of Justinian had ever asserted this doctrine of absolutism quite as unequivocally as he.

6. *Geschichte der Staatsrechtswissenschaft*, pp. 149–150.

7. Edouard Cuq, *Les institutions juridiques des Romains* (1904), vol. I, p. xxiv.

8. *Geist des römischen Rechts*, vol. I, title 1, chap. 2, sec. 18.

9. *Loc. cit.*

10. *Dissertations on Early Law and Custom*, p. 389.

11. *Digest*, 2, 15, 14.

12. *Digest*, 1, 7, 34.

13. *Digest*, 2, 14, 7, 5.

14. *Institutiones*, III, 145.

15. *Ibid.*, p. 146.

16. *Digest*, 1, 3, 1. In the next fragment of the same title, from the *Institutions* of Marcianus, an extract is given in Greek from a supposed oration of Demosthenes in which *lex* is defined as πόλεως συνθήκη κοινή; and some have thought that the words of Papinian are a mere paraphrase of this definition. It does not seem to me probable.

17. *Digest*, 35, 2, 1, pr.

18. II, 249.

19. *Digest*, I, 3, 31.

20. *English Law and the Renaissance*, Cambridge, 1901.

21. *Doctor and Student*, Dialogue I, chap. 5.

22. This was apparently the first sentence of the *Institutiones* of Gaius. The single surviving manuscript of Gaius is defective in the beginning and does not include these words, but in the corresponding part of the *Institutes* of Justinian the whole paragraph of which this is the first sentence is quoted

verbatim from the extract from Gaius in the *Digest* (I, 1, 9). The paragraph is the first in the Gaius manuscript, and its lost first sentence may therefore be supplied without hesitation from the *Digest*. It is likely that Saint-German knew it, if at all—and he probably did know it—from its inclusion in the *Institutes* of Justinian.

23. F. W. Maitland, *Select Passages from the Works of Bracton and Azo* (Selden Society), p. xiv.

24. ". . . car chascuns barons est souverains en sa baronie" (Beaumanoir, *Coutumes de Beauvaisis*, II, 1043 [p. 23]).

25. "La maxime *princeps legibus solutus est* dans l'ancien droit public francais," in *Essays in Legal History*, ed. by Paul Vinogradoff (Oxford, 1913), pp. 201 ff.

26. *Ibid.*, p. 204.

27. For Vacarius, see C. F. C. Wenck, *Magister Vacarius Primus Juris Romani in Anglia Professor* (Lipsiae, 1820); F. de Zulueta (editor), *The Liber Pauperum of Vacarius* (Selden Society), 1927.

28. This distinction here so clearly made between *leges* and *consuetudines* refers, I think, to the difference between enactments and customs. The *peritia juris* of the next sentence refers to the law or "right" involved in particular cases, and the *consuetudo regni* immediately following it has reference to the feudal *consilium* due from tenants in chief in the *Curia Regis*, sanctioned by a feudal customary law common in the whole realm. The old English translation of John Beames is very misleading here. He translates the words above, *in peritia juris et regni consuetudinibus*, "in skill in the Law and Customs of the Realm," reading *consuetudinibus* as though it were *consuetudinum* and thus confusing and distorting the whole meaning and constitutional significance.

29. Leges namque Anglicanas licet non scriptas leges appellari non videatur absurdum, cum hoc ipsum lex sit, quod principi placet legis habet vigorem, eas scilicet quas super dubiis in concilio definiendis, procerum quidem consilio et principis accedente auctoritate constat esse promulgatas.

30. *Digest*, I, 3, 32.

31. *Chronicon Monasterii de Abingdon* (Rolls Series), I, 297. It seems probable, from the details he gives, that the chronicler may have been an actual witness of what he records here, for the account must have been written soon after 1185; the chronicle itself ends in 1189. Although allowance must be made for the author's natural bias, this is not likely to have affected the correctness of the most significant words in his quotation from the Chief Justiciar.

CHAPTER IV (pages 67–92)

1. F. W. Maitland, *Bracton's Note Book*, I, 9–10. See also his introduction to *Select Passages from the Works of Bracton and Azo*.

2. Maitland, *Bracton's Note Book*, I, 30–33. Maitland thinks this *addicio*

may possibly have been made by Bracton himself after the completion of the body of his treatise, but in any case Maitland is also clear that it contradicts other statements made at least five times in all parts of the book. To me it is those other statements, and not this one, that give us the true indication of the political views of Bracton himself and the majority of men in his time. I concur heartily with Dr. Kantorowicz against Maitland, in the former's higher estimate of Bracton's knowledge and understanding of Roman law, though possibly for reasons somewhat different from his; but I cannot agree that "no passage more genuinely Bractonian" than this one "stands in the whole treatise" (H. Kantorowicz, *Bractonian Problems* [Glasgow, 1941], pp. 49–52). The important and revolutionary ideas of Dr. Kantorowicz respecting the date and authorship of the Bractonian text are only remotely related to the question of Bracton's constitutionalism, and are therefore not discussed here. On pages 78, 89, and elsewhere I have retained the date of Bracton's Treatise preferred by Güterbock and Maitland. For criticisms of the theories of Dr. Kantorowicz, see Professor G. E. Woodbine, "Bractonian Problems," in *Yale Law Journal,* LII (March, 1943), 428–444; Fritz Schulz, "Critical Studies on Bracton's Treatise," in *Law Quarterly Review,* LIX (April, 1943), 172–180. I have discussed the views of Dr. Kantorowicz more at length in "The Present Status of the Problem of the Bracton Text," in *Harvard Law Review,* LVII (December, 1943). See also Fritz Schulz, "Bracton on Kingship," in *English Historical Review,* LX (May, 1945), 136–176.

3. Ante, p. 50, *Digest,* I, 3, 1; Bracton *De Legibus et Consuetudinibus Angliae,* folio 2 A (ed. by George E. Woodbine [New Haven, 1922], II, 22).

4. ". . . et est loi commun plégen de toute commun chose" (*Li livres de jostice et de plet,* ed. Rapetti, p. 4).

5. Folio 1.

6. *Digest,* I, 4, 1; *Inst.,* I, 2, 6.

7. Folio 107.

8. Arthur Taylor, *The Glory of Regality* (London, 1820), p. 410.

9. This passage of Bracton was commented on with great learning by John Selden (*Ad Fletam Dissertatio,* cap. iii, § ii), who, according to Hallam (*Middle Ages,* chap. ix, part ii), "extenuated the effect of Bracton's predilection for the maxims of Roman jurisprudence." Maitland seems to agree substantially with Selden, but regards Bracton's variation from Justinian "rather a playful perversity than a mistake" (*Bracton's Note Book,* I, 4, note 2). My interpretation does not vary materially from that of Selden and Maitland, except that I fail to see anything "playful" in the passage. It has been criticized by Dr. Ludwik Ehrlich (*Proceedings Against the Crown* [Oxford Studies in Social and Legal History], ed. by Sir Paul Vinogradoff, VI, 39, note 3).

There is no doubt that Bracton's *cum* is a preposition in the text as we have it. This, however, is only to say on the evidence of that text that Bracton consciously *altered* Justinian's statement, whether seriously or "playfully." It is *not* to say that he *misunderstood* it. In fact, although the *cum* is undoubtedly

158

a preposition in the existing text, I am inclined to believe that this in itself is no sufficient proof that Bracton necessarily thought of the original as such. If he had been preparing this statement for a modern printer he might well have included the words *cum lege regia* within quotation marks. He could scarcely quote verbatim Justinian's legalized despotism in support of his own conception of government limited in its scope by law. As Professor Schulz well says, "He [Bracton] ought to have written 'etc.' after 'est,' or," as he adds somewhat less convincingly, "perhaps he did write it" (*English Historical Review,* LX, 155).

10. Folio 54.

11. Folio 5. For some practical illustrations of these principles, see the excellent little book by Professor A. B. White, *Self-Government at the King's Command* (Minneapolis, Minn., 1933).

12. Howell's *State Trials,* III, cols. 28, 49.

13. Folio 55 B ff.

14. *De Regimine Principum,* Book III, part 2, chap. vi.

15. *Reliquiae Spelmannianae,* p. 57, *English Works* (London, 1727).

16. Matthew Paris, *Chronica Majora* (Rolls Series), III, 75–76.

17. Stubbs, *Select Charters,* 9th ed., p. 350.

18. *Ibid.,* pp. 395–397.

19. *Ibid.,* pp. 407–411.

20. *Ibid.,* p. 396.

21. Folio 55 B. In form perhaps this is consciously reminiscent of Justinian's phrase, *quod ad singulorum utilitatem pertinet* (*Institutes,* I, 1, 3), as an antithesis to it.

22. Folio 1 B.

23. *Chronicon Monasterii de Bello* (London, 1846), pp. 65–67.

24. *De Necessariis Observantiis Scaccarii Dialogus,* ed. by Hughes, Crump, and Johnson (Oxford, 1932), p. 139.

25. Stubbs, *Select Charters,* 9th ed., p. 173.

26. Ante, p. 75.

27. Ante, p. 65.

28. Ante, pp. 81–82.

29. *The Case of Proclamations,* 8 James I, 12 *Rep.,* p. 75.

30. *The Governance of England,* ed. by Charles Plummer (Oxford, 1885), introduction, p. 83.

31. *Chapters in the Administrative History of Mediaeval England,* V, 61.

32. "Le corps de tout le Royalme," the words of Chief Justice Thorpe in the Bishop of Chichester's Case (Year Book, Easter Term, 39 Edward III).

33. *English Constitutional Ideas in the Fifteenth Century* (Cambridge, 1936). See also Professor T. F. T. Plucknett, *The Lancastrian Constitution* (*Tudor Studies,* ed. by R. W. Seton-Watson; London, 1924), pp. 161–181; C. H. McIlwain, *The Growth of Political Thought in the West* (New York, 1932), pp. 354–363; and the admirable new critical edition of Fortescue's

De Laudibus Legum Angliae, ed. by Dr. S. B. Chrimes (Cambridge, 1942), the first edition to be based on all the known manuscripts.

34. *Religion and the Rise of Capitalism,* p. 102.

35. In I, II, and III *Codicis Libros Commentaria* (Venice, 1615), folio 64, cited by A. Lemaire, *Les lois fondamentales de la monarchie française* (Paris, 1907), p. 41, note.

36. On the Continent, the transition from the medieval theory of *dominium* to the modern theory of sovereignty—the theoretical concomitant of the development of the modern nation-state—was made largely in the form of a changing interpretation of the *merum et mixtum imperium et jurisdictio* of the Roman law sources. The contemporary discussions of these all-important terms in the period between the thirteenth and the seventeenth century are fundamental and very numerous but they have been used amazingly little by the historians of political thought. Bracton's discrimination between *gubernaculum* and *jurisdictio* might be called the English equivalent of these discussions; but Bracton came too early to develop his distinction fully, and his successors in England lacked the knowledge of Roman law and the interest in it which so color and control all continental treatments of the same important political problems. It has been necessary here to confine attention to the English side of this development alone. This, however, seems to show that Cowell was historically correct, and Coke wrong, when the former asserted, early in the seventeenth century, that the English common law *nihil aliud esse quam Romani & feudalis mistionem* (*Institutiones Juris Anglicani,* Authore Johanne Cowello [Oxford, 1664], "Epistola Dedicatoria"; first published in 1605). For similar views about the Roman element in English law expressed by Lord Ellesmere, see his speech in the case of the Post-Nati (Howell's *State Trials,* II, 673). For the continental side, reference might be made to Mr. C. S. N. Woolf's *Bartolus of Sassoferrato* (Cambridge, England, 1913), which deals with an early stage of the development; and for the later stages, to the volume by Mr. Myron P. Gilmore, *Argument from Roman Law in Political Theory 1200–1600* (Harvard Historical Monographs, Cambridge, Mass., 1941). I can now include also the admirable study of Mr. William Farr Church, *Constitutional Thought in Sixteenth-Century France* (Harvard Historical Studies, Cambridge, Mass., 1941).

CHAPTER V (pages 93–122)

1. *The Whole Workes of W. Tyndall, John Frith, and Doct. Barnes* (London, 1573), pp. 111–118, *passim.* On the general subject of the early Tudor monarchy and the contemporary theories concerning it, see *The Early Tudor Theory of Kingship,* by Franklin Le Van Baumer (New Haven, 1940); *Early Tudor Government, Henry VII,* by Kenneth Pickthorn (Cambridge, 1934).

2. Commentary on the Book of Daniel, *Works,* V, 91.

3. *De Justa Henrici Tertii Abdicatione e Francorum Regno Libri Quatuor,* Parisiis, 1589.

4. ". . . *Iesuits* are nothing but Puritan-papists" (*A Premonition*, *Political Works of James I*, p. 126).

5. Cited by A. Lemaire, *Les lois fondamentales de la monarchie française*, p. 58.

6. "Et neantmoins demeure tousiours la dignité & auctorité royalle en son entier, non pas totalement absolue, ne aussy restraincte par trop, mais reglée & refrenée par bonnes loix, ordonnances & coustumes, lesquelles sont establies de telle sorte qu'a peine se peuuent rompre & adnichiler, iaçoit qu'en quelque temps & en quelque endroit, il y aduienne quelque infraction & violence. Et pour parler desdictz freins par lesquelz la puissance absoluë des Roys de France est reglée, i'eu treuue trois principaulx, Le premier est la religion, Le second la iustice, Et le tiers la police." Chap. viii, folios 9–10. "Le second frein est la iustice, laquelle sans point de difficulté est plus auctorisée en France qu'en nul autre païs du monde que lon sçache, mesmement à cause des parlements qui ont esté instituez principalement pour ceste cause, & à ceste fin de refrener la puissance absoluë dont vouldroient vser les Roys" (Claude de Seyssel, *La grand' monarchie de France* [Paris, 1558], chap. x, folio 11; first edition, 1519).

7. *De l'estat et succez des affaires de France* (Paris, 1571), p. 82.

8. *The Letters of Stephen Gardiner*, ed. by James Arthur Muller (New York, 1933), p. 370.

9. *Ibid.*, p. 377.

10. *Ibid.*, pp. 379 ff.

11. Quoted by Thomas McCrie, *Life of John Knox*, note BB.

12. *Eight Centuries of Reports*, by Judge Jenkins (1734), Fourth Century, Case XCIII.

13. *Ibid.*, Sixth Century, Case XXXV, 23 Elizabeth.

14. *Ibid.*, Seventh Century, Case LXXXIII, 2 James I.

15. *Ibid.*, Fourth Century, Case XXXVI, 1 Henry VII.

16. *Ibid.*, Fifth Century, Case XXVII, 34 Henry VIII.

17. *Anderson's Reports*, I, 152, translated in Thayer's *Cases on Constitutional Law*, I, pp. 12–15.

18. *A Compleat Journal of the Votes, Speeches and Debates, both of the House of Lords and House of Commons Throughout the Whole Reign of Queen Elizabeth, of Glorious Memory*, collected by . . . Sir Simonds D'Ewes, Baronet (London, 1693), p. 633. For the unfavorable estimate of the character of Serjeant Heyl, Hele, or Heale, by Lord Ellesmere, himself no enemy of the royal prerogative, see Lord Campbell's *Lives of the Lord Chancellors and Keepers of the Great Seal of England* (2d ed.; London, 1846), II, 207–210. In a case before the Star Chamber in 1604, Lord Ellesmere voted to "find him [Hele] guilty in all of corruption and ambition, craft and covetous practices," and apparently he was fined 1,000 pounds (*Les Reportes del Cases in Camera Stellata*, ed. by W. P. Baildon [1894], pp. 171–176, 411). See also *The Egerton Papers* (Camden Society, 1840), pp. 315, 391, 399; *Lives of*

Eminent Serjeants-at-Law, by Humphry William Woolrych (London, 1869), I, 172–185.

19. *Ibid.,* p. 640.

20. *England in the Reign of King Henry the Eighth* (Early English Text Society), pp. 100–101.

21. For a convenient though abridged text of the Statute of Proclamations, see *Tudor Constitutional Documents,* ed. by J. R. Tanner, p. 532; for the circumstances of the passing of the act, Dr. Tanner's introductory note (pp. 529–532), and the article by Professor E. R. Adair, in *English Historical Review,* XXXII, 34–46.

22. *A History of England from the Defeat of the Armada to the Death of Elizabeth,* II, 275.

23. *Introduction to Political Science,* p. 256.

24. *Ibid.,* pp. 253–254. While this is true for most of the time as a matter of form after the enactment of the Triennial Act in 1664, and a parliament was usually in being, parliament's effectiveness was not secured till means were found to ensure a session as well as an election, and such means were not found till the Revolution. The unprecedented number of prorogations and dictated adjournments in the reigns of Charles II and James II were as effective as a dissolution in checking any parliamentary opposition to the Crown. In 1677 Buckingham and Shaftesbury argued that such prorogations if they lasted more than one year were equivalent to a dissolution under the provisions of two unrepealed statutes of Edward III. For this Shaftesbury was put in prison at the pleasure of the Lords *and the King,* where he remained for more than a year and was then released only on a full renunciation of his error. The Tudor monarchs had met the growing opposition of parliament by subjugating their parliaments, a method progressively less and less effective. The Stuart method came to be one by suppression rather than subjugation when subjugation failed, and Charles I succeeded in this policy till the Scottish war forced his hand. After the Restoration Charles II was not faced with the problem until the later sessions of the long Cavalier Parliament and its successors. He then followed his father's method, but by prorogation instead of flat violation of the Triennial Act of 1664. Before his death, however, he was forced to violate his own statute. James II, in the single parliament called by him, returned to his brother's earlier method of suppression through prorogation.

25. *Parliamentary History,* I, 555.

26. In the old English translation of the Latin original (Pierre Janelle, *Obedience in Church and State* [Cambridge, 1930], p. 93).

27. D'Ewes, *Journal,* p. 12.

28. *Ibid.,* p. 151.

29. *Ibid.,* p. 141.

30. *Ibid.,* p. 168.

31. *Ibid.,* p. 175.

32. *Ibid.*, p. 185.

33. *Ibid.*, p. 244.

34. *Ibid.*, pp. 284–285.

35. *Ibid.*, p. 460. The italics are mine. These matters are referred to later in the same parliament as "matters of State, or Causes Ecclesiastical" (*ibid.*, p. 479).

36. *Ibid.*, p. 470.

37. The phrase of Sir Humphrey Gilbert on 1571 (*ibid.*, p. 168).

38. *The Prerogative of Parliaments* (1644), Harleian Miscellany (ed. of 1745), V, 208.

39. 1 Jac. I, cap. 1; *Statutes of the Realm,* IV, 1017.

40. The king's speech in parliament in 1607 (*The Political Works of James I* (Cambridge, Mass., 1918), p. 300.

41. *De Republica Anglorum,* ed. by L. Alston (Cambridge, 1906), book II, chap. ii, p. 58.

42. *The Trew Law of Free Monarchies* in *The Political Works of James I,* p. 62.

43. Speech of 1605 (*ibid.*, p. 288).

44. *Parliamentary History,* I, 1326–1327.

45. *Ibid.*, I, 1344.

46. *Ibid.*, I, 1351. For a penetrating analysis of the constitutional struggle in England between 1603 and 1649, see *The Royal Prerogative, 1603–1649* by Francis D. Wormuth (Ithaca, N.Y., 1939).

47. *Commons Debates, 1621,* ed. by Notestein, Relf, and Simpson (New Haven, 1935), V, 239.

48. *Ibid.*, p. 240.

49. Willion v. Berkley, *Plowden's Commentaries,* pp. 236–237.

50. *Commons Debates, 1621,* II, 490.

51. Ante, p. 44 *et seq.*

52. Ante, p. 69.

53. Ante, p. 70.

54. Palgrave, *Parliamentary Writs* I (Anno XXIII Regis Edwardi, p. 30).

55. *Rot. Parl.*, II, 290 A. Qe le dit Roi Johan ne nul autre purra mettre lui ne son Roialme ne son Poeple en tiele subjection, saunz Assent & accorde de eux.

56. Rex v. the Bishop of Chichester, Year Book Pasch. 39 Edward III, p. 7.

57. Year Book Pasch. 19 Henry VI, no. 1; Plucknett, *The Lancastrian Constitution, Tudor Studies,* ed. by R. W. Seton-Watson, p. 163.

58. Wimbish v. Tailbois, 4 Edward VI, *Plowden's Reports,* p. 59. For reference to this interesting case I am indebted to the unpublished thesis of Mr. Edward T. Lampson, *The Royal Prerogative, 1485–1603,* in the Harvard University Library. Mr. Lampson has now published an interesting analysis and discussion of this important case: "Some New Light on the Growth of Parliamentary Sovereignty: Wimbish versus Taillebois," *American Political*

Science Review, XXXV (October, 1941), 952–960. For some discussion of the earlier English cases dealing with this matter, see Brinton Coxe, *An Essay on Judicial Power and Unconstitutional Legislation* (Philadelphia, 1893), pp. 147–164; *A Discourse upon the Exposicion and Understandinge of Statutes,* by Samuel E. Thorne (San Marino, California, 1942). On the general subject of the expropriation of private property, see also my *Growth of Political Thought in the West,* p. 181, note 2, and p. 190, note 1, with the references there cited, especially the valuable paper by E. Meynial, "Notes sur la formation de la théorie du domaine divisé," in *Mélanges Fitting* (Montpellier, 1908), II, 409–461. The political principles vaguely touched on in Wimbish v. Taillebois became the basis of the long struggle between ruler sovereignty and popular sovereignty and of the antithesis between the constitutional limits possible under the former and the illimitable power of the people. The persistence of this fundamental conflict is well illustrated by the antagonistic views of Thomas Jefferson on the one side and those of Chief Justice Marshall and Mr. Justice Story on the other. See "The Story-Marshall Correspondence (1819–1831)" by Charles Warren, *William and Mary College Quarterly,* 2d ser., XXI, no. 1 (January, 1941). Thus Jefferson wrote in 1820: "When the legislative or executive functionaries act unconstitutionally, they are responsible to the people in their elective capacity. The exemption of the judges from that is quite dangerous enough. I know no safe depository of the ultimate powers of society but the people themselves; and if we think them not enlightened enough to exercise their control with a wholesome discretion, the remedy is not to take it from them, but to inform their discretion by education. This is the true corrective of abuses of constitutional power." In a letter from Story to Marshall of June 27, 1821, the former writes: "Mr. Jefferson . . . in the most direct terms denies the right of the Judges to decide constitutional questions . . . and endeavours to establish that the people are the only proper Judges of violations of constitutional authority and by changes in the course of election are alone competent to apply the proper remedy. If, he says, it is objected they are not sufficiently enlightened to exercise this duty with discretion, the remedy is to enlighten them the more. . . . There never was a period of my life when these opinions would not have shocked me, but *at his age,* and in these critical times, they fill me alternately with indignation and melancholy. Can he wish yet to have influence enough to destroy the government of his Country?"

59. See Appendix, post, pp. 170 ff.

60. *De Republica Anglorum,* ed. by Alston, p. 105.

61. *Ibid.,* p. 106.

62. *Ibid.,* p. 104.

63. *The Third Part of the Institutes of the Laws of England* (1644), p. 35.

64. The evidence is collected in David Jardine's valuable *Reading on the Use of Torture in the Criminal Law of England Previously to the Commonwealth* (1837), and many instances are given in *A History of Crime in Eng-*

land, by Luke Owen Pike, 2 vols., London, 1873, 1876. See also Sir William Holdsworth, *A History of English Law,* Vol. V (1924), pp. 184–188. The most recent work on this subject is *The History of Torture in England* by L. A. Parry, but it adds little to our knowledge of the subject and nothing to our understanding of its constitutional implications.

65. Jardine, *A Reading on the Use of Torture,* p. 16.

66. Howell's State Trials, II, 871.

67. *Jardine,* p. 24.

68. *Ibid.,* Appendix 15.

69. Holdsworth, *History of English Law,* V, 185.

70. II *State Trials,* 774, note.

71. Jardine, p. 59.

72. *History of England,* Vol. VI, p. 359, n. 2. See also Holdsworth, *History of English Law,* V, 186.

73. John Selden, *Table Talk,* s. v. *Tryalls.*

74. For discussions of the oath Ex Officio and its constitutional importance, see R. G. Usher, *The Reconstruction of the English Church* (1910); *The Rise and Fall of the High Commission* (1913); Mary Hume Maguire, *Attack of the Common Lawyers on the Oath Ex Officio as Administered in the Ecclesiastical Courts in England,* in *Essays in History and Political Theory in Honor of Charles Howard McIlwain* (1936), pp. 199–229; [Richard Cosin], *An Apologie for Sundrie Proceedings by Iurisdiction Ecclesiasticall* (1593); [James Morice,] *A briefe treatise of Oathes exacted by Ordinaries and Ecclesiasticall Iudges, to answere generallie to all such Articles or Interrogatories, as pleaseth them to propound. And of their forced and constrained Oathes ex officio, wherein is proved that the same is unlawful; The Argument of Master Nicholas Fuller, in the case of Thomas Lad, and Richard Maunsell, his Clients, Wherein it is plainely proved, that the Ecclesiasticall Commissioners have no power, by vertue of their Commission to Imprison, to put to the Oath Ex Officio, or to fine any of his Maiesties Subjects,* Imprinted 1607. The book of Cosin is an elaborate defense of the procedure of the Commissioners, approximately one-third of which is devoted to the Ex Officio oath and to the attack on it in Morice's book and in one other anonymous writing of the time. Mrs. Maguire refers also to *A Collection shewinge what iurisdiction the Clergie hath heretofore lawfully used and may lawfully use in ye Realme of England* (Calthorpe MSS., Vol. 44, folios 99–202), another attack on the methods of the commissioners, by Robert Beale, which I have not seen.

75. For the illustration of the dispensing power, see Paul Birdsall, *"Non Obstante"—A Study of the Dispensing Power of English Kings,* in *Essays in History and Political Theory in Honor of Charles Howard McIlwain,* pp. 37–76.

76. D'Ewes, *Journal,* p. 547.

77. *Acts of the Privy Council,* New Series, Vol. 32, p. 237; *State Papers Domestic,* Elizabeth, Vol. 82, no. 8.

78. *The Case of Monopolies,* XI Coke's *Reports,* 84. The case is reported

also in the *Reports* of Noy and Moore. See Cheyney, *History of England*, II, 306–308; W. H. Price, *The English Patents of Monopoly* (Harvard Economic Studies), pp. 22–24; *Select Charters of Trading Companies* (Selden Society), ed. by Cecil T. Carr, Introduction, p. lxvi; J. W. Gordon, *Monopolies by Patents* (1897), especially app. II (pp. 193–232); Sir William Holdsworth, *A History of English Law*, IV (1924), 343–354; D. Seaborne Davies, "Further Light on the Case of Monopolies," *Law Quarterly Review*, no. 48 (July, 1932), pp. 394–414.

79. Townshend's *Historical Collections* (1680), p. 239.

80. *Ibid.*, p. 249.

81. Proclamation of November 28, 1601. Price, *The English Patents of Monopoly*, app. J (pp. 156–159). The historians of the constitution have dwelt upon Elizabeth's suppression of actual monopolies, which she did by her mere prerogative. It is far more significant that subjects injured by the monopolies *allowed to remain* were here declared to have "their liberty to take their ordinary remedy by her Highness's laws of this realm." Similar provisions occur in the subsequent proclamations of James I and in the Statute of 1624. But Charles I characteristically preferred to act in such matters "of his mere grace and favor" and "by his regal power" wherever he was able to do so. It may be said without exaggeration that this fundamental power claimed as of right by the king, to stay any action involving the royal prerogative in the lower courts of common law or any debate touching it in "The High Court of Parliament," is in practice the real crux of the whole constitutional struggle of the sixteenth century in England. The "Prerogative Royall may not be called in question"; yet, since the time of Henry VIII, by the common lawyers, it had been "made a great matter, the stay of the Common Lawe," as Stephen Gardiner wrote to the Protector Somerset in 1547. See also *Original Letters Illustrative of English History*, ed. by Sir Henry Ellis, 3d ser., IV, 87–90, (London, 1846), a letter to the Lord Chancellor and Lord Treasurer written apparently in 1591 and signed by eleven judges of the common-law courts, the whole of the three benches except Baron Sotherton, complaining, among other things, that "divers have bene imprisoned for sueinge ordinarie accōns and sutes att the common lawe untill they will leave the same, or, againste theire matter to order, althoughe sometime yt be after judgmente and execucōn."

CHAPTER VI (pages 123–146)

1. Report of Barbaro in *Calendar of State Papers Venetian*, V, 341.

2. Howell's *State Trials*, II, 389. This distinction between the two kinds of power exercised by the king was indicated clearly by Alberico Gentile: "Atque absoluta potestas est plenitudo potestatis. Est arbitrio plenitudo, nulli vel necessitati, vel iuris publici regulis subiecta, quod ex Baldo acceptum dicunt alii. est potestas extraordinaria, et libera. est illa, quam in Anglia significamus nomine *regiae Praerogativae*. Atque sic interpretes iuris communiter scribunt,

esse in principe potestatem duplicem, ordinariam adstrictam legibus, et absolutam definiunt, secundum quam potest ille tollere ius alienum, etiam magnum, etiam sine caussa" (Alberici Gentilis J.C. Professoris Regii, *Regales Disputationes Tres:* id est, De potestate Regis absoluta, Londini, 1605, pp. 10–11). The late Sir William Holdsworth considered such a characterization of the English king as "an absolute ruler" a proof of Bodin's inaccuracy (*A History of English Law,* vol. IV, p. 194). If this is an inaccuracy, however, it is one that Bodin shared with most of the jurists and practically all of the statesmen in England in his time. Thus, for example, Richard Bancroft speaks of "the freest and most absolute monarchies" (*Daungerous Positions and Proceedings,* 1593, book I, chap. 6); Sir Walter Raleigh, in the preface to his *History of the World,* says that Philip II "attempted to make himself not only an absolute monarch, like unto the Kings of England and France, but Turk like, to tread under his feet all their natural and fundamental laws, privileges, and ancient rights"; and even Sir Edward Coke proved to his own entire satisfaction "that the Kingdom of England *is an absolute monarchy,* and that the King is the only supreme governor as well over ecclesiastical persons, and in ecclesiastical causes, as temporal within this realm" (*5th Reports,* xii). Likewise, in his instructions to the grand jury for the trial of the regicides in 1660, Sir Orlando Bridgeman, Chief Baron of the Exchequer, asserted that "this is an absolute monarchy." But, he added, "It is one thing to have an absolute monarchy, another thing to have that government absolutely without laws" (*State Trials,* V, 991–992). Other instances are not infrequent in the interval. As Locke said, "Even absolute power, when it is necessary, is not arbitrary by being absolute" (*Two Treatises of Government,* book II, chap. xi). Bodin's use of the word "absolute" in referring to the English monarchy seems to be fully warranted by contemporary usage in England itself, but his interpretation of this, derived as he says from the Civilian, Dr. Valentine Dale, then English ambassador to France, is, I admit, rather extreme for that time on the side of the prerogative (*Les six livres de la République,* Paris, 1577, p. 102). For Bodin, however, "absolute" does not imply the entire absence of legal limitations, and his theory, though exceptional, is not unique; for Dale was not the only English Civilian who held the same. In fact, a few English royalists of the time—and not all of them Civilians—went considerably beyond Bodin, in holding that the king had authority to take subsidies without consent. After 1642 there were more of these in England, after 1649 probably many more.

3. "There is a Prerogative disputable and a Prerogative indisputable, as to make warre and Peace; the other concerns *meum et tuum* and are bounded by Lawe" (Pym's Diary, *Commons Debates,* 1621, ed. by Notestein, Relf, and Simpson, IV, 79).

4. Howell's *State Trials,* III, 1083.

5. Speech in the Star Chamber, 1616, *The Political Works of James I,* p. 333.

CONSTITUTIONALISM

6. *A Dialogue of the Common Law, The English Works of Thomas Hobbes,* ed. by Molesworth, VI, 12.

7. *State Trials,* II, 371.

8. *Ibid.,* p. 559.

9. *Ibid.,* III, 1. The speeches of Digges, Littleton, Selden, and Coke concerning this case, delivered before a committee of the Lords and Commons in 1628, were published in London in 1642.

10. *State Trials,* III, 825.

11. *Ibid.,* II, 396.

12. *Ibid.,* III, 36–37.

13. *Ibid.,* p. 45.

14. *Ibid.,* p. 46.

15. *State Trials,* III, 174.

16. *Ibid.,* p. 62.

17. *Ibid.,* p. 173.

18. *Ibid.,* p. 185.

19. *Ibid.,* p. 193.

20. *Ibid.,* p. 79.

21. *Ibid.,* p. 194.

22. *Ibid.,* pp. 193–194.

23. *Ibid.,* p. 66.

24. As put by Selden (*State Trials,* III, 170).

25. *Ibid.,* p. 57.

26. *Ibid.,* p. 78.

27. For the violent language of Edward Hyde, afterwards earl of Clarendon, against these judges, used in the first session of the Long Parliament in 1640, see *ibid.,* p. 1282.

28. *A History of the Custom-Revenue in England* (1892), I, 17.

29. Even so late and so extreme an upholder of royal authority, divine right, and passive obedience as Sir George MacKenzie acknowledged that private property was ordinarily outside the scope of the king's lawful authority: "For it is fit to know, that Government is the Kings, and Property is the Subjects Birth-right. Monarchy is a Government, and so can include no more than what is necessary for Government. And though the *Turk* or *Mogol,* arrogate to themselves, the total property of their Subjects, in this they are Tyrants, and not Kings. And when our Statute above-mentioned, says, *That our Kings have as much power as they,* this is only to be understood of what Right they have by the Nature of Monarchy, *Rex nomen est jurisdictionis non dominii,* say the Lawyers" (*Jus Regium* [London, 1684], pp. 50–51). He holds that "our Parliaments are not co-ordinate with our Kings, in the *Legislative* Power; but that the *Legislative* and *Architectonick* Power of making Laws (as lawyers term it) does solely reside in the King, the Estates of Parliament only consenting" (p. 67). And yet he has to admit that "what is once ours, cannot be taken away without consent" (p. 51). This is in practice almost precisely

168

the position of Bodin and of other great French jurists of his time. By the seventeenth century, however, most of them had come to agree with the more absolutistic view of Le Bret when he recognized a right in the French Kings, undeniable even if only prescriptive, *"d'user absolument de leur authorité, et de leuer sur leurs peuples des Tailles et des subsides; mesmes sans leur consentement"* (*De la souveraineté du Roy,* par messire Car. Le Bret, Conseiller ordinaire de sa majesté en ses Conseils d'Estat & Prive [Paris, 1632], p. 396). Nothing could better illustrate the growing fundamental difference between the modern development of constitutional principles in France and in England; the great practical importance of "the power of the purse" in accounting for that difference; or the significance of the persistence in England of the definition of the rights to private property in a Common law determinable by judges or the High Court of Parliament only, and not by the King apart from the estates, which made "the power of the purse" ultimately an effective means of securing and maintaining constitutional limitations upon the exercise of arbitrary government in any fields whatsoever. The power to tax involves the power to destroy, and often to destroy—or to control—much more than the thing directly taxed.

30. *The Constitutional History of England* (New York, 1897), I, 314.

31. *Ibid.,* I, 378.

32. Andrew Amos, *The English Constitution in the Reign of King Charles the Second* (1857), p. 11.

33. Printed for the first time in 1924. See Holdsworth, *History of English Law,* V, app. III.

34. Hargrave MSS, no. 94, f. 14 (British Museum).

35. *Op. cit.* In his *Reflections* on Hobbes's *Dialogue,* Hale deals with the *potestas irritans* more briefly but to the same effect: "3 Potestas Irritans, and thus the Laws also in many cases bindes ye Kinges Acts, and make them void if they are agt Lawe" (Holdsworth, *History of English Law,* V, III, p. 508).

36. *State Trials,* III, 1017.

37. Sir Robert Berkley in the Ship-Money Case (*ibid.,* III, 1099).

38. *State Trials,* III, 1083.

39. Holdsworth, *A History of English Law,* V, 508.

40. Coke's *Reports,* XI, 84.

41. *State Trials,* III, 1125.

42. 21 & 22 Jac. I, cap. 3.

43. *Certayne Considerations upon the Government of England* (Camden Society), p. 10.

Appendix

In the last session of the Reformation Parliament in 1536 two remarkable statutes were enacted truly revolutionary in character, the Statute of Uses with which the above case of Wimbish v. Tailbois is concerned, and the act transferring to the Crown the property of the lesser monasteries. Both these acts involve an invasion of private right by parliament almost, if not entirely, without precedent before 1536 and far more revolutionary than the Statute of Proclamations enacted by a subsequent parliament three years later, which has been called "the English *Lex Regia*" and termed even by Maitland "the most extraordinary act in the Statute Book" (*The Constitutional History of England*, p. 253). These two statutes of 1536 therefore mark an important early stage in the developments which led in the course of time to the constitutional doctrine of parliament's omnipotence and the modern theory of legislative sovereignty.

In the reign of Edward II Parliament had, it is true, transferred from the reversioners to the Hospitallers lands formerly belonging to the Templars; but this was only some years after Pope Clement V had totally suppressed the Order of the Templars in his bull *Vox in excelso*, and the transfer was expressly said by the Judges and Council to be "for the Health of their Souls and Discharge of their Consciences," because these lands had originally been granted for pious uses only, and "insomuch as the foresaid Order of the Templars is ceased and dissolved, and the foresaid Order of the Hospital is provided, instituted, and canonized for the defence of Christians" (17 Edward II, stat. II, 1323–4, *Statutes of the Realm*, I, 194 ff.). This was in essence a judicial decision based on a principle closely analogous to the *Cyprès* doctrine of the later courts of Equity. Doubts of the statute's validity seem to have persisted however, for in 1330 there was a petition in parliament praying for its annulment on the ground that it had been obtained by the Despencers by force, and was *"contre Ley et contre reson"* (*Rot. Parl.* II, 41–42). In the king's *responsio* to this petition the matter was reserved for action in a later parliament, but no record of any such action is known. During the Hundred Years' War parliament had also dealt in a somewhat similar way with the lands of the alien priories.

As encroachments upon private right and departures from common law by mere authority of parliament, these and all such earlier cases, however, fall considerably short of the act of 1536, in which the Lords and Commons "humbly desire the King's Highness that it may be enacted *by authority of this present Parliament,* that his Majesty shall have and enjoy to him and his heirs forever" all the lands and goods of monastic houses not having revenues above 200 pounds a year (27 Henry VIII, C.28, *Statutes of the Realm,* III, p. 575 ff.); an act directed not against "alien" houses, and not in time of war. For the bad eminence as "the most extraordinary act in the Statute Book," I should therefore be inclined to nominate this revolutionary act of 1536, expropriating the lands of the lesser monasteries, in place of the usual greatly limited and short-lived Statute of Proclamations, enacted by a later and apparently somewhat less subservient parliament; at least if contemporary rather than modern standards are to be taken into account. The story told by Sir Henry Spelman of the pressure required to secure the passage of this statute seems not improbable. The bill had originated with the King himself, and not with the Commons (F. C. Dietz, *English Government Finance 1485–1558,* University of Illinois Studies in the Social Sciences, vol. IX, no. 3, 1920, p. 120); and, as Spelman reports the tradition, "It is true the Parliament did give them [the lesser monasteries] to him, but so unwillingly (as I have heard), that when the Bill had stuck long in the lower house, and

171

could get no passage, he [the King] commanded the Commons to attend him in the forenoon in his gallery, where he let them wait till late in the afternoon, and then coming out of his chamber, walking a turn or two amongst them, and looking angrily on them, first on the one side, then on the other, at last, I hear (saith he) that my Bill will not pass; but I will have it pass, or I will have some of your heads: and without other rhetoric or persuasion returned to his chamber. Enough was said, the Bill passed, and all was given him as he desired" (*The History and Fate of Sacrilege,* ed. of 1895, p. 99).

In an earlier session of the Reformation Parliament an ominous prelude to the Act of Dissolution appears in the preamble to the statute of 1534 (25 Henry VIII, chap. 21, *Statutes of the Realm,* III, 464), concerning Peter's Pence and papal dispensations, in which it is declared, that "It standeth therefore with natural Equity and good Reason, that in all and every such laws human made within this Realm, or induced into this Realm by the said Sufferance, Consents and Custom, your Royal Majesty, and your Lords Spiritual and Temporal, and Commons, *representing the whole State of your Realm,* in this your most high Court of Parliament, have *full Power and Authority,* not only to dispense, but also to authorize some elect Person or Persons to dispense with those, *and all other human Laws of this your Realm,* and with every one of them, as the Quality of the Persons and Matter shall require; and also *the said Laws, and every of them, to abrogate, annul, amplify or diminish, as it shall be seen unto your Majesty, and the Nobles and Commons of your Realm present in your Parliament, meet and convenient for the Wealth of your Realm.*" This, however, is only a preamble; and "the object of Tudor preambles," as Dr. Tanner says, "is not to tell the truth but to make out a case." The enacting clauses themselves "abrogate" no provisions which their makers professed to regard as true law, but only such as were termed usurpations or involved an "unlawful paiment." Notwithstanding this sweeping inclusion in the preamble of all human laws, this statute, therefore, constitutes no revolutionary break with the past comparable with the act of dissolution two years later, but its remarkable language is a no less interesting indication of men's changing notions concerning the relation of government to law. It is noteworthy that the legislative power here claimed for parliament is a power not directly to make new law, but to annul, enlarge, or restrict the old. Such preambles as these were not alone apologies for the specific enactment immediately following: they were part of the royal propaganda to ensure the passage of more drastic legislation in the future. The startling character of that propaganda proves alike the newness of the proposals made and to be made and the opposition to them to be expected.

Hardly less revolutionary than the Act of Dissolution was the contemporary proposal which failed of enactment, for setting up a new court of "Conservators" with jurisdiction in cases where "anye persone or persones shall chaunce at any tyme hereaftir within any Counties or liberties of this Realme or within any other place of any of the King our soueraine lordis dominions as well in and vpon lande as in or vpon any watirs freshe or Salte to doo or tattempte any devise practice or experience whiche hathe bene is or in tyme to come shal be thought vnto the said Conservatours to bee hurtefull or preiudiciall to the Comon Weale of this Realme, and none Acte, statute prouysion or ordynaunce made for Refourmacion of the same" (*Transactions of the Royal Historical Society,* 4th ser. XIX [1936], 143–144). This provision, if it had become law, would have rivaled in arbitrariness the German Penal Code Amendment Law of 1935 authorizing the Courts to punish as offences acts which no law had ever forbidden. See, on the general principles involved in this proposed legislation, the admirable article of Professor Jerome Hall, "Nulla Poena sine Lege," *Yale Law Journal,* XLVII, no. 2 (December, 1937).

The legality of the Act of Dissolution and of similar "legislation" was unquestionably a matter of some doubt in the minds of the lawyers of the time. In 1532 Christopher Saint German declared in his *Treatise concernynge the division betwene the spiritualtie and temporaltie:* "It is holden by them that be lerned in the lawe of this royalme, that the parlyamente hath an absolute power as to the possession of all temporall thynges within this realme, in whose handes so ever they be, spiritualle or temporalle, to take them froo one manne, and gyve theym to an nother withoute anye cause or consideration. For if they doo it, it byndeth in the lawe" (*The Apologye of Syr Thomas More Knyght,* ed. by Arthur Irving Taft, Early English Text Society, London, 1930, app., p. 228).

To this assertion of the absolute power of parliament, Sir Thomas More gave the following answer: "But by what right men maye take awaye from any man spyrytuall or temporall agaynste hys wyll, the lande that is al redy hys owne that thynge thys pacyfyer [Saint German] telleth vs not yet. . . . But I have herde some good and wyse and well lerned men saye, that all the worlde can neuer brynge the reason that euer can preuve it ryghte. . . . For all be it that onys in the tyme of the famouse prynce kyng Henry the fourth, aboute the tyme of a greate rumble that the heretykes made, whan they wolde have destroyed not the clergye onely but the kynge also and hys nobylbte to there was a folysshe byll and a false put into a parleament or twayn, and spedde as they were wurthy: yet had I neuer founden in all my tyme whyle I was conuersaunt in the courte, of all the nobylytie of thys land aboue the nomber of seuen (of whyche seuyn there are now thre dede) that euer I perceyued to be of the mynde, that it were eyther ryght or reasonable, or could be to the realme profytable without lawful cause, to take any possesyons awaye from the clergy, whyche good and holy prynces and other deuoute vertuouse people, of whome there be now many blessed sayntes in heuen, have of deuocyon towards god geuyn to the clergy to serve god and praye for all Chrysten soulys" (*op. cit.,* pp. 86–94).

Further evidence of the doubts existing in the reign of Henry VIII concerning the authority of parliament thus to "legislate" appears in the elaborate preparations for the act of dissolution, in

174

the visitations, the reports of the visitors, and the long apologetic preamble to the statute itself, reciting the monastic abuses found and piously attributing the statute to the King's reforming zeal in "daily finding and devizing the increase, advancement, and exaltation of true doctrine and virtue in the said Church, to the only glory and honour of God and the total extirping and destruction of vice and sin." For hypocrisy and studied mendacity this preamble has but one rival, the preamble which the government felt it necessary to prefix to the statute of 1539 ratifying the dissolution of the larger monasteries. The act of 1536 had contemplated sending inmates of the dissolved smaller houses to live in the larger, "considering also that divers and great solemn monasteries of this realm wherein, thanks be to God, religion is right well kept and observed, be destitute of such full numbers of religious persons as they ought and may keep." After that admission it was difficult even for Henry VIII to attempt a direct dissolution of the larger houses, on the former pretext of "manifest sin, vicious, carnal, and abominable living," and therefore it is asserted in the preamble of the act of 1539, flatly contrary to fact, that these larger houses had surrendered all their lands and goods to "our said Sovereign Lord, his heirs and successors for ever," "of their own free and voluntary minds, good wills, and assents, without constraint, coaction, or compulsion of any manner of person or persons . . . by due order and course of the common laws of this his realm of England, and by their sufficient writings of record under their convent and common seals" (31 Henry VIII, c. 13, *Statutes of the Realm,* III, 733). The truth is, as Dugdale says, that the monks of these larger monasteries were induced to surrender their houses to the King "partly through corrupting the chief in each of them, with large pensions, during their lives: and partly by terror, to such as were not plyant" (*The Baronage of England* [London, 1675], I, *The Preface*).

The uncertainty as to parliament's inherent authority to violate rights guaranteed by earlier law thus indicated is also reflected in the comments of Sir Edward Coke upon the procedure by bill of attainder in the case of Thomas Cromwell in 1540. In the section on the High Court of Parliament in his Fourth Institute, he says, "And albeit I finde an attainder by Parliament of a subject of High Treason being committed to the Tower, and forth-comming to be heard, and yet never called to answer in any of the Houses of Parliament, although I question not the power of the Parliament, for without question the attainder standeth of force in law; yet this I say of the manner of the proceeding, *Auferat oblivio, si potest; si non, utcumque silentium tegat:* for the more high and absolute the jurisdiction of the court is, the more just and honourable it ought to be in the proceeding, and to give example of justice to inferiour Courts. But it is demanded, since he [Cromwell] was attainted by Parliament, what should be the reason that our Historians do all agree in this, that he suffered death by a law which he himselfe had made. For answer hereof, I had it of Sir Thomas Gawdye Knight, a grave and reverend Judge of the King's Bench who lived at that time, that King Henry VIII commanded him to atend the chiefe Justices, and to know whether a man that was forth-comming might be attainted of High Treason by Parliament and never called to his answer. The Judges answered, that it was a dangerous question, and that the High Court of Parliament ought to give examples to inferiour Courts for proceeding according to justice, and no inferiour Court could do the like; and they thought that the High Court of Parliament would never do it. But being by expresse commandement of the King and pressed by the said Earle [Cromwell] to give a direct answer: they said that if he be attainted by Parliament, it could not come in question afterwards, whether he were called or not called to answer. And albeit their opinion was according to law, yet might they have made a better answer, for by the Statutes of *Mag. Cart.* ca. 29, 5E. 3, cap. 9 et 28E. 3, cap. 5. No man ought to be condemned without answer . . . which they might have certified, but *facta tenent multa quae fieri prohibentur;* the act of Attainder being passed by Parliament, did bind, as they resolved. The party against whom this was in-

176

tended was never called in question, but the first man after the said resolution that was so attainted, and never called to answer, was the said Earl of Essex. . . . The rehearsall of the said Attainder can work no prejudice for that I am confidently perswaded that such honourable and worthy members shall be from time to time of both Houses of Parliament, as never any such Attainder where the party is forth comming, shall be had hereafter without hearing of him" (*The Fourth Part of the Institutes of the Laws of England*, pp. 37–38).

Facta tenent multa, quae fieri prohibentur, says Coke, quoting a current maxim which apparently paraphrases a dictum of Innocent III from the Decretals of Gregory IX, III, 31, 16: "quia multa fieri prohibentur, quae si facta fuerint, obtinent firmitatem." But if so, in all probability another maxim of the law was no less prominent in his mind: non firmatur tractu temporis, quod de jure ab initio non subsistit: *Liber Sextus Decretalium de Bonifacii Papae VIII, V, 12, De Regulis Juris, Regula xviii;* or the words of Paulus from which it was derived: Quod initio vitiosum est, non potest tractu temporis convalescere (*Dig.,* 50, 17 [*De Diversis Regulis Juris Antiqui*] 29). "Many things which have been done are binding although they are forbidden to be done!" Coke as well as the judges to whom he refers, seems, on the whole, to be thinking here of parliament in its judicial rather than its legislative capacity; as the *dernier resort,* the body from whose decision there is no appeal, even though wrong. Except for his too modern characterization of parliamentary attainder as an act of "legislative power," the interpretation of this statement of Coke's by Sir John Hawles, Solicitor General, author of the celebrated *Englishman's Right,* in the great case of Sir John Fenwick in 1696, the last English attainder in a capital case, seems to be entirely sound: "The truth is, it hath been the irregular Proceedings in obtaining those Acts have been blamed, and not the making use of the Legislative Power for that purpose; and therefore consider the Acts of Attainder mentioned by the Council, which have been blamed, and first, that of my *Lord*

Cromwel which my Lord *Coke* blames: One of the Council at the Bar pretended to repeat my Lord *Coke's* Words of that Matter at large; but he did not deal so candidly with you in that matter as he ought to have done; for he should have repeated all my Lord *Coke* says on that Subject, which was, That *Cromwel* was never brought to answer, never permitted to say any thing for himself, either in Parliament or elsewhere, and for that Reason alone my Lord *Coke* blames that Precedent" (*The Proceedings Against Sir John Fenwick, Bar. upon a Bill of Attainder for High Treason*, printed in the year, 1702, p. 207; Howell's *State Trials*, XIII, 666, where the statement is somewhat abridged).

From Coke's own emphasis in his comments it is apparent that he considered a parliamentary attainder as a *judgment* of the highest of all courts, a judicial procedure warranted by the famous clause of Edward III's Statute of Treasons, which, after the definition of certain specific acts as treason actionable in the courts below, goes on to provide "That if any other Case supposed Treason, which is not above specified, doth happen before any Justices, the Justices shall tarry without any going to Judgement of the Treason till the Cause be shewed and declared before the King and his Parliament whether it ought to be judged Treason or other Felony" (25 Edw. III, Stat. 5, c.2, I *Statutes of the Realm*, p. 320).

Two or three years after the enactment of the statute the parliamentary attainder of Roger Mortimer was annulled *en plein Parlement* as *erroignes & defectives en touz pointz,* solely on the ground that *le dit Counte estoit mys a la mort & desherite sanz nul Accusement & sanz estre mesne en Juggement ou en Respons* (*Rot. Parl.* 28 Edw. III, no. 11 [vol. II, p. 256]).

In view of such precedents Sir Edward Coke evidently regarded a parliamentary attainder as a procedure at the common law, and *for this reason* condemned Cromwell's attainder for lack of "due process," because the accused was "forthcomming to be heard, and yet never called to answer." "For that reason alone my Lord Coke blames that precedent." The validity of a "legislative" act would not be affected whether the accused were "forthcoming" or not, nor by any other defect of "due process." It was probably for the same general reason that Coke, unlike Wentworth, insisted on going by petition instead of by bill in the Petition of Right in 1628. (See *The Petition of Right*, by Frances Helen Relf, Minneapolis, 1917, pp. 27–43).

This passage from the *Fourth Institute* may also serve to make somewhat clearer the meaning of Coke's well-known and much debated assertion in Dr. Bonham's case that "in many cases the common law will controul acts of Parliament, and sometimes adjudge them to be utterly void" (8 *Reports*, 118). It may be worth noting that the Earl of Shaftesbury, a former Lord Chancelor, made a similar statement in 1677: "This Court [The King's Bench] will, and ought to judge an Act of Parliament null and void if it be against Magna Charta" (*A Life of Anthony Ashley Cooper, First Earl of Shaftesbury*, by W. D. Christie, London, 1871, vol. II, app. VI, p. XCV). Bonham's case is not an assertion of the supremacy of natural law or of judicial discretion: it is the *common law*, and it alone, that "will controul acts of parliament." On the general question whether the above clause of Edward III's statute was regarded by later English jurists as referring to judicial or to legislative action, see my *High Court of Parliament* (New Haven, 1910), chap. III, note A (pp. 247–248).

Such a collision of royal will, embodied in Cromwell's case in an act of parliament, with the prohibitions of the law, in the sixteenth century is reminiscent of similar occurrences in England in the middle ages referred to above on page 83, and somewhat analogous to the French *lit de justice*. The Tudor monarchs were strong enough to prevail in such a contest, and it is not strange that Henry VIII could say, some two years after Cromwell's attainder, that "we at no time stand so high in our estate royal as in the time of parliament"; but it was not to remain so in the future, and the ultimate outcome of the long struggle was to be a supremacy in parliament of a kind which few or none of the earlier combatants

179

had ever envisaged. Yet it was the Reformation Parliament, impelled by pressure from the King, that brought about the greatest break with medieval ideas of law and government and initiated the intellectual movement which culminated later in the constitutional doctrine of the omnipotence of Parliament and the modern theory of legislative sovereignty.